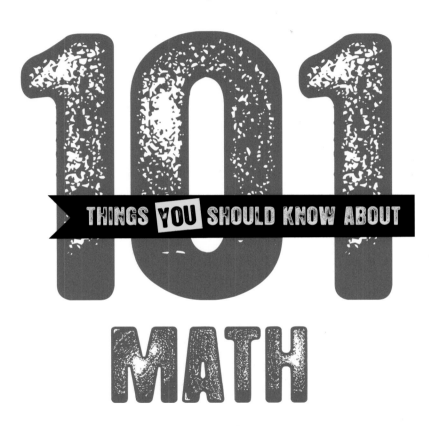

101

THINGS YOU SHOULD KNOW ABOUT

MATH

STERLING
New York

An Imprint of Sterling Publishing
387 Part Avenue South
New York, NY 10016

ISBN 978-1-4549-1043-5

Distributed in Canada by Sterling Publishing
c/o Canadian Manda Group, 165 Dufferin Street
Toronto, Ontario, Canada M6K 3H6
Distributed in the United Kingdom by GMC Distribution Services
Castle Place, 166 High Street, Lewes, East Sussex, England BN7 1XU
Distributed in Australia by Capricorn Link (Australia) Pty. Ltd.
P.O. Box 704, Windsor, NSW 2756, Australia

For information about custom editions, special sales, and premium and corporate
purchases, please contact Sterling Special Sales at 800-805-5489 or
specialsales@sterlingpublishing.com.

For Pulp Media Limited:
AUTHOR: Sonia Mehta (in association with Quadrum Solutions)
SERIES ART DIRECTOR: Allen Boe
SERIES EDITOR: Helena Caldon
DESIGN & EDITING: Quadrum Solutions
PUBLISHER: James Tavendale

IMAGES courtesy of www.shutterstock.com

Manufactured in China

2 4 6 8 10 9 7 5 3 1

www.sterlingpublishing.com

Banana Seed Books

Gift for Mrs. Fine's 4th grade

From Dylan Levine

Date 2015

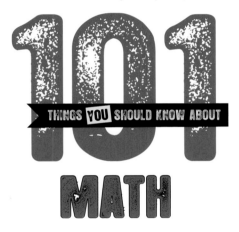

101

THINGS YOU SHOULD KNOW ABOUT

MATH

STERLING

New York

INTRODUCTION

Let's travel into the complex and versatile world of mathematics. This book takes you through a journey of over 101 extremely interesting facts about math. As German mathematician Georg Cantor once accurately said, "The beauty of mathematics lies in its freedom." Its principles are universally applicable for various purposes. Mathematics is actually a way of life! It becomes a part of us from the day we start counting our fingers. Every morning, when we look at the clock, we are unknowingly utilizing our knowledge of math!

The foundation of mathematics begins with numbers and shapes, which we use on a daily basis. Whether we are number crunching in our heads while calculating the grocery bill or keeping track of the points during a game, we are using mathematical knowledge.

As we go through the history of mathematics and come across the measurement of time, we get to know how man invented numbers and came up with calendars. Great mathematicians and intellectual tricks have shaped mathematics and made it easier for the rest of us. This book will definitely leave you spellbound when you discover the beauty of numbers and witness how mathematics impacts every part of our daily lives.

INFINITE

NUMERALS

NEGATIVE NUMBERS

ABACUS

DIVIDER

NUMBER SYSTEM

CALCULATE

VALUE

MATHEMATICIAN

THE HISTORY
OF MATH

ONE

INTEGERS

ZERO

1. THE FIRST NUMBER

The history behind the origin of numbers is a huge mystery. However, it is certain that numbers have immensely molded the development and civilization of the human race. We use numbers in almost every daily activity. Can you imagine what life would be like without numbers?

At first, prehistoric people counted by carving the number one repeatedly in wood, bone, or stone. This is how they accounted for days and counted things. This shows that the history of mathematics began in the same way that we begin learning numbers today – with the number "one!" However, it was not referred to as "one" back then; it was represented in the exact same way that we represent it today – with a single vertical line. Historians and mathematicians have been able to collect concrete evidence which clearly indicates that the number "one" was first used about 20,000 years ago in the African region of Congo.

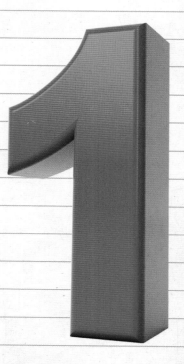

The Ishango Bone

The discovery of the "Ishango Bone" led historians and mathematicians to this conclusion. The Ishango Bone, found in Congo, Africa, is the fibula bone of a baboon, which is roughly 20,000 years old. It has a uniform series of straight lines carved on it. These represent the number "one." Further research has helped conclude that they used it to represent a certain number of objects, things, dates, etc.

FAST FACT . . .
The Ishango bone is preserved at the Royal Belgium Institute of Natural Science in Brussels, Belgium.

The Ishango Bone

2. THE FIRST CURRENCY

Though the earliest evidence of numbers dates back to around 20,000 years, it is widely believed that numbers only gained importance once civilizations became more complex and cultures were developed. As the number of material possessions and belongings increased, it became essential to keep an account of everything.

The use of numbers and counting gained significance almost 4,000 years ago. Evidence of a complex system of counting and numbers was first discovered in Sumeria, the capital of the Mesopotamian civilization. Being the most

populous cities of its times, it followed a system of counting to keep tabs of all things used, traded or added to inventories. The Sumerians maintained a series of tokens, each of which represented some object or item that could be traded, used, or given to someone else.
The tokens were clay cones, which were kept in pouches. When the number of objects began increasing exponentially, the Sumerians realized that there was no need to have separate tokens for everything. They replaced this counting method with clay tablets on which a mark was added or removed for every object taken or given away respectively.

This marked not just the beginning of mathematics, but also the birth of currency and money.

FAST FACT . . .
A famous mathematician by the name of Henri Poincare once said, "Mathematics is the art of giving the same name to different things." He is probably quite right, as everything in mathematics is interrelated.

3. EGYPTIAN MEASURES

Until the rise of the ancient Egyptian civilization around 3000 B.C., units of measurement were not well-defined. The Egyptians not only came up with a relatively accurate system of measurement, but also developed symbols to represent different numbers. Their advanced system of arithmetic and mathematics helped them build legendary structures like the Pyramids of Giza.

The Egyptians gave the number "one" a completely new meaning. Apart from using it for counting purposes, they transformed "one" into a unit of measurement as well.

The number "one" was used as a unit of length.
The Egyptians also came up with symbols for representing different numbers.

The representative symbol of the number "one" was a simple straight line also used by Africans in Congo 20,000 years ago. A rope was the symbol for the number "ten." A coil of rope represented the number "100." Similarly, they had symbols for higher numbers like thousand and ten thousand too.

The Cubit

The Egyptians invented the cubit, which became their standard unit of measurement. It was derived from the number "one." It was approximately equal to the length of a man's forearm, from his elbow to fingertips, including the width of his palm. The cubit was considered sacred and official. A stick used to represent it was kept in Egyptian temples with new ones being made from the original sticks. This prevented any errors in measurement.

FAST FACT . . .

The Egyptians had remarkable mathematical knowledge thousands of years ago. This assisted them in building gigantic structures that are still intact! Amazing Egyptian constructions such as the Great Pyramids of Giza and the Sphinx are among the seven wonders of the world and are astounding pieces of architecture.

4. THE ZERO HEROES

The entire concept of possessing "nothing" or "nought" has been an implicit part of mathematical understanding since ancient times. However, it was not until the number "zero" was invented that this concept was actually converted into an important part of arithmetic and mathematics.

The invention of the number "zero" is considered to be one of the most monumental strides in the progress of mathematics. The number "zero" is found to have first appeared around the fifth century A.D. Complex calculations were only possible post its discovery. Until then, only counting was possible. Once zero was discovered, fields like trigonometry, algebra, and calculus developed. Zero gave mathematics a way to represent "nought" and quantifying it. If "zero" was never invented, computers would never have been invented either! So possessing "nothing" doesn't seem that bad anymore, does it?

Who Invented Zero?

It is widely believed that the Babylonians, Mayans, and Indians independently invented "zero." Some mathematicians like Robert Kaplan are of the opinion that a pair of angled wedges were used to represent

FAST FACT . . .

The credit for the real development of the number zero has been given to the Indians. Around 458 A.D., Indian mathematician Brahmagupta developed a symbol for "zero," which was a dot underneath numbers. Since then, the concept of "zero" spread to China, the Middle East, and all parts of the world.

"nothing" or "zero" in earlier times by the Sumerians of Mesopotamia around 4,000 years ago. This method then passed on to the Babylonians. Initially, they left empty spaces to represent "nothing" but on realizing that this was causing confusion, they also started using two angled wedges to represent the concept of "nought."

5. BABYLONIAN NUMBERS

The Babylonian number system is one of the first well-developed number systems. It was used for hundreds of years until it was succeeded by the Hindu-Arabic number system. Among some of its salient features, a striking one was the importance of the number "sixty," which was an important base for calculation.

No other number system before or after the Babylonian number system has used "60" in the same way. The Babylonian number system came into existence around 1800 B.C., and was derived from the numbers and counting systems of their predecessors, the Sumerians or Mesopotamians.

FAST FACT . . .
The number sixty served as a base in the Babylonian number system, like the way we use the number "one" today. For example, the number "three hundred" was represented by five "sixties."

Basic Working
The Babylonians represented their numbers by engraving them onto clay tablets with a stylus. The number "one" was not a straight line. It represented a stylus (a straight line with an inverted triangle on top).

In order to represent numbers from 2 to 9, they used a combination of "ones" or styluses. Thus two was represented with two "ones" and so on. However, the "ones" were neatly arranged into piles,

which were quite unique.
To represent the number "ten,"
they turned the stylus on to its
side. 20 was represented by two
"tens" and so on.
A combination of "ones" and
"tens" were used to represent
any number up to "60".

FAST FACT . . .

Babylonian mathematics
did not have any concept
of regular multiplication
like we use today. Since
they had a sexagesimal
system that was to the
base of 60, all they needed
to do was know the
squares of the numbers.
By knowing the squares
and the table of squares,
they used another method
of multiplication that
involved the addition and
subtraction of squares.

FAST FACT . . .

Babylonian mathematicians
were very advanced for
their times. It is believed
that they had come up
with a primitive and
fairly accurate version of
Pythagoras Theorem long
before Pythagoras
was born!

6. THE MAYAN SYSTEM

The Mayan civilization treated the number "zero" differently. Even though it was not used for making mathematical calculations, zero was an important part of their number system.

The ancient Mayans of South America devised an interesting number system that was primarily used to keep track of time. It helped them count days according to the 360-day lunar calendar that they followed. In fact, the entire place value system of the Mayan number system was also designed to help the Mayans keep track of time.

0	1	2	3	4
5	6	7	8	9
10	11	12	13	14
15	16	17	18	19

FAST FACT . . .
According to the Mayans, the world started on August 11, 3114 B.C., which is the date their calendar starts from.

Most numbers were based on three symbols , which were used to represent the numbers "zero," "one," and "five" respectively. "Zero" was represented with a shell, "one" was represented with a dot, and five was represented with a straight line. "Zero," "one," and "five" were physically represented by a shell, pebble, and stick respectively. These objects were a part of their counting process. Combinations of these three symbols were used to represent different numbers while following the place value system.

For example, the number "22" was represented by a pebble in the second place and two sticks in the first place.

FAST FACT . . .

Did you know that Egyptians were not the only ones to build pyramids? People belonging to the Mayan and Aztec civilizations also built pyramids. Many of them were much larger than the Pyramids of Giza! This can be credited to their tremendous understanding of mathematics.

The Mayan Pyramids

7. THE BIRTH OF INTEGERS

Integers are the set of all positive and negative whole numbers, including zero. Integers do not include decimals or fractions. They have been responsible for the developments of several mathematical concepts. As obvious as the concept of integers might seem, they were never defined accurately until just a few centuries ago.

Although it is commonly believed that integers were among the first numeric systems developed by our forefathers for counting, this was actually not the case. It was only later that the concept of integers was developed. Evidence of the existence of integers was first seen in the mathematics practiced by the Babylonians. Not only did they develop

with the concept of integers. Though human beings knew how to count and did so even 20,000 years ago, they did not know what they were counting. It was not possible for them to further develop concepts like subtraction and multiplication. The birth of integers helped them understand what was being counted and develop fields like algebra and geometry.

a fixed system of numbers, but they also knew how to add and subtract. Once, their mathematical developments were passed on to the Greeks, the number system was revolutionized. They helped develop the field of algebra and started solving whole number equations. Diophantus of Alexandria developed this system of solving equations using whole numbers around 250 A.D.

During the Renaissance period, the Europeans made new breakthroughs in mathematics

FAST FACT . . .

The negative of a negative number is always positive. The positive of a negative number and the negative of a positive number are always negative. The positive of a positive number is always positive.

-(+) = -
+(-) = -
-(-) = +
+ (+) = +

8. THE INFINITE CONCEPT

One of the most interesting mathematical concepts is that of infinity. It is derived from the Latin word "infinitas" meaning "unbounded." Interestingly, even though the concept of infinity was not so well-developed in ancient times, certain civilizations had an intuitive understanding of this concept and even considered it to be a part of their number system.

Even in modern times, a lot of questions related to infinity remain unanswered. It is represented by the symbol shown alongside. Infinity is a term used to refer to something that has no limit. In mathematics, infinity is used to count things which have no bounds or can go on to a value that cannot really be counted. For example, the size of the entire universe is considered to be "infinite," as it is believed to have no bounds. Even the entire set of integers is considered to be an "infinite" set as there is no end point.

Ancient Greeks and Indians

Ancient Greek and Indian civilizations were unable to convert the concept of "infinity" into a mathematical concept. The ancient Greeks were the first to have come up with the idea of "infinity." Anaximander of Miletus coined the term "apeiron," which means limitless or boundless. Zeno of Elea and the great Aristotle further developed the concept of infinity.

The ancient Indians however, seemed to have a much better mathematical understanding of the concept of infinity. This concept is mentioned in writings that date back around 1000 B.C.

FAST FACT . . .
George Cantor was the first to officially propose the theory of "infinity" in 1890. His theory was criticized at first, but is now known as one of the foundations of modern mathematics.

George Cantor

9. THE EGYPTIAN DIVIDERS

A very monumental step in the development of mathematics is the birth of division. Addition, subtraction, and multiplication were known to man thousands of years ago. However, division as we know today is a little more complicated. The Egyptians were the first to lay down a systematic format of division!

The Egyptian Procedure of Division

The Egyptian division system was slightly complex and could only be applied to certain numbers and smaller values. They used multiplication to divide things. Division played a very important role in their culture, as it was crucial for building their wonderful architectural marvels.

Their method is best understood through an example. Let's see how they divided 62 by the number 7.

They kept doubling 7 up to the number closest to 62.
So 7 x 2=14 x2=28 x 2=56. They realized that 7 multiplied by 8 equals 56 which was close to 62. They then subtracted 62 from 56 to get 6 as the answer which they approximated to 7. Hence 62 divided by 8 was 8 times 7 plus one more 7 which is 9 times 7. This is how they carried out division, which was actually a modified form of multiplication.

FAST FACT . . .

One of the major reasons why the Great Pyramids of Giza are still marvelous and almost perfectly intact even today is that the Egyptians had advanced knowledge on the field of geometry. They could accurately calculate the angle of the pyramid's slope and also perfectly carve thousands of rectangular blocks in equal sizes without any machines!

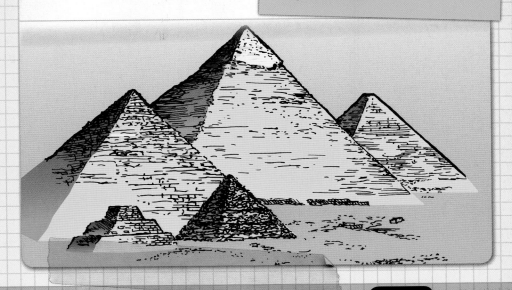

10. HINDU-ARABIC NUMERALS

The Hindu Arabic numeral system is among the earliest number systems and closest to the one we use. Having originated from the "Brahmi" numerals of ancient Indians, it is believed to be the first decimal number system. It was also the first system to give the number "ten" a crucial role in the place value system.

The Hindu-Arabic numerals are believed to have originated in India. They have been derived from the Brahmi numerals around the eighth or ninth century A.D. The Brahmi numerals were a well-developed number system with different symbols for different numbers. The decimal place value system was not a part of it, but became an important part of the Hindu-Arabic number system. It spread to the Middle East from India, and it was the Arabs who introduced this system to Europe. Hence, it is popularly referred to as the Hindu-Arabic number system.

The Hindu-Arabic number system is simpler than the Mayan and Babylonian systems. It uses the number "ten" as a base number. Hence, it is called

Arabic numbers

the decimal system. Distinct symbols were used to represent numbers from "zero" to "nine." This system grouped "tens" to represent higher numbers and numbers from 10 onwards were representing the second place in the decimal system. Thus, to represent 10, the symbol of one was used in the second place and the symbol of zero was used in the first place. This concept is followed by us even today!

FAST FACT . . .

The symbols that we use to represent numbers like 1, 2, and 3 today are based on the Hindu-Arabic Numeral System, which is thousands of years old. Numbers were considered to be best developed in this numeral system.

11. THE ROMAN NUMERALS

Roman Numerals are commonly used even today in number lists and other numeric forms. Having been developed during the times of the powerful Roman Empire, they have stood the test of time. Though Roman numerals are used even today, the number system that was followed by them turned extinct during the Roman Empire itself.

The use of Roman numerals started with the beginning of the Roman Empire. Roman numerals like I, II and IV are seen in the Latin Palatine Hill and are believed to have been created around the eighth century B.C. Roman numerals are commonly used even today.

In its early times, the Roman Empire flourished thanks to philosophers and traders who needed to keep an account of things. The Roman number system was developed from their predecessors, the Greeks. Great mathematicians like Euclid, Aristotle, and

Archimedes helped devise several mathematical theorems which are used even today. It was their

I   II   III   IV   V
VI   VII   VIII   IX   X
XI   XII

progress in mathematics which led to the construction of huge and wondrous monuments like the Colosseum, Constantine's Arch, and the Roman Baths.

Roman Numerals in Modern Times

Roman numerals are actually a combination of different letters. Numbers from 1 to 10 are represented as I, II, III, IV, V, VI, VII, VIII, IX, and X respectively. The unique concept about this system is the way they represented large numbers. They used different letters for larger numbers, like L for 50, C for 100, D for 500, and M for 1000.

FAST FACT . . .

Roman numerals are often used to distinguish between generations of people from the same family. Many royal families use the same name repeatedly in their lineage. For example, there were 8 King Henrys in the United Kingdom through the ancient and medieval times. Roman numerals from 1 to 8 were put after their name to distinguish between them, for example, King Henry VIII.

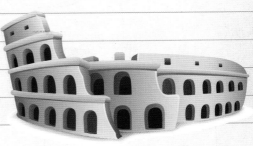

12. NEGATIVE NUMBERS

For a long time, negative numbers did not exist. In fact, Egyptian and Greek civilizations considered negative numbers to be absurd! It was the Indians and the Chinese who eventually developed negative numbers and filled a glaring void in mathematics. After the birth of negative numbers, it was possible to solve a lot of equations that were considered false until then!

Chinese Pioneers

The first appearance of negative numbers in any historical text has been found in the book "Nine Chapters on the Mathematical Art," written around 100 B.C., during the time of the Han dynasty. An interesting method was used by them to indicate negative numbers. Black counting rods indicated negative numbers while red counting rods represented positive numbers. If you notice, this is exactly the opposite of what happens in today's times.

Indian Pioneers

Being pioneers in the field of mathematics, early Indians were not just well-versed with the concept of negative numbers but also applied their knowledge to develop various other fields of mathematics. They developed consistent and accurate rules for working with negative numbers which are applied even today. Calculations were carried out using negative numbers in ancient Indian texts like the "Bakhshali Manuscript." Back then, "+" was used as a negative sign! Around the seventh century A.D., Indian mathematician Brahmagupta wrote "Brahma-Sphuta-Siddhanta," in which he discussed the use of negative numbers in detail and also found negative solutions for quadratic equations. He formulated the rules for banking. Back then, negative numbers were used to indicate debt.

FAST FACT . . .
The negative value of a negative number is a positive number. For example − (-8) = +8.

13. THE ABACUS

The abacus is a basic counting device. It was made popular by ancient merchants and traders. It was also used to carry out simple mathematical operations like addition and subtraction. Even though its significance has reduced, it has survived the tests of time and is used today to teach students the art of counting.

The word "abacus" is a Latin word derived from the Greek word "abax" or "abakon" meaning "table" or "tablet." From the Salamis tablet of abacus used around 300 B.C. to the present day Soraban Abacus; this instrument has a very colorful history! Ancient people began using sticks, stones and pebbles for higher numbers. When they fell short of such sticks and stones to count larger numbers, they realized that they needed a better method to count. This is when the abacus was created. The uniform feature of all abaci is that they have different numbers of beads placed on

different lines or rods, each of which depict a particular place value (units, tens, hundreds, etc.). The earliest abacus ever found is the Salamis Tablet used by the Babylonians in around 300 B.C. From then on, the abacus underwent various transformations through the ancient, medieval, and modern times.

The abacus was initially made of stones and metals. The modern day abacus is a Japanese Soraban Abacus with one bead in the upper deck and five in the lower deck. It is an important tool that is used to help young children learn how to count.

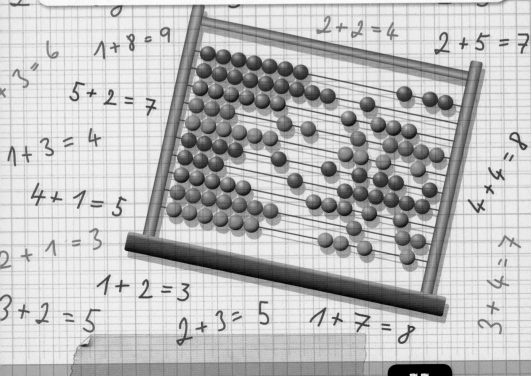

2

$3 = 6$

$1 + 8 = 9$

$2 + 2 = 4$

$2 + 5 = 7$

$5 + 2 = 7$

$1 + 3 = 4$

$4 + 4 = 8$

$4 + 1 = 5$

$2 + 1 = 3$

$4 = 7$

$1 + 2 = 3$

$3 + 2 = 5$

$2 + 3 = 5$

$1 + 7 = 8$

$3 +$

YEARS

SUN DIAL

UNIT

DIALS

MONTHS

SECONDS

THE MATH OF
MEASURING TIME

14. CHINESE CALENDAR

The ancient Chinese calendar is among the most complex calendars known to mankind and is continuously undergoing changes even today! Like most other ancient calendars, the Chinese calendar is also a solar-lunar calendar.

MOON PHASES

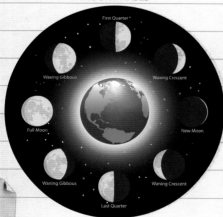

The biggest complication in this calendar is that its date of commencement has been reset numerous times.

Every time a new ruling dynasty took over the Chinese empire in ancient times, the date of commencement was changed. Additionally, the ancient Chinese calendar is continuously modified based on new astronomical findings. Imagine looking at a calendar whose dates continue to change!

The months in a solar-lunar calendar are set according to the cycles of the moon, while the years are set according to the solar year. Since the lunar year is approximately 354 days while the solar year is around 365 days, there is a slight difference between the two.

The Sexagesimal Cycle

One of the most important features of the Chinese calendar, which also inspired the Japanese calendar, is the "sexagesimal" or "sexagenerian" cycle. This is basically a 60 year cycle. It is a combination of 10 celestial bodies or heavenly stems called "tian gan" and 12 earthly branches called "di zhi." Each of these 12 earthly branches corresponds to a certain animal. Hence, we often hear about the Chinese year of the dog, the year of the bull, etc. Each of these gets repeated every 12 years.

FAST FACT . . .

The oldest time-keeping machine is believed to have been invented by the Chinese. It was called the "gnomon" and is today popularly known as the "Sun Dial."

15. THE JAPANESE CALENDAR

The Japanese have followed a lunar-solar calendar for over 13 centuries. Even though it is inspired by the Chinese calendar, the Japanese calendar is unique in many ways. Most Japanese traditions and festivals are based on their calendar.

Around 13 centuries ago, Korean priest Kanroku developed the Japanese lunar-solar calendar. Japanese months were based on it from 604 A.D. to 1873 A.D., until they finally adopted the commonly used solar calendar of 365 days.

Chinese Influence

The Japanese calendar shared many similarities with the Chinese calendar. A striking similarity was their method of designating years. They based it on their Royal rulers. Thus, every period of a certain set of years corresponded to the period of reign of a certain King or monarch. It was called a "nengo period." Another prominent similarity is that the calendar had a 12-year zodiacal cycle. Each year in a 12 year cycle, called "jūnshi," corresponded to a certain animal.

Intercalary Months

Each month in the Japanese lunar-solar calendar was either 29 days or 30 days long. The short and long months were not fixed and varied based on religious reasons. As the lunar year was only 354 days long and the solar year was 365 days long, every third year had an additional month called the intercalary month. This was added to adjust the lunar calendar and bring it in sync with the solar year.

FAST FACT . . .

Japanese mathematics is based on the "soraban," which is the Japanese version of the abacus. The soraban is a commonly used form of the abacus in most parts of the world today. It is used for advanced computation with incredible accuracy.

16. THE ROMAN CALENDAR

The Roman calendar, which was followed during the early years of establishment of the Roman Empire, was quite strange in numerous ways. The original Roman calendar did not account for the months of January or February at all!

The Roman calendar is also referred to as the "pre-Julian" calendar. It consisted of hollow months that were shorter months of 29 days, and full months with longer months of 30 days. The Roman calendar also had a different system of numbering the days in a month. The months were divided into three day markers based on the position of the moon.

It is believed that Romulus, the first king of Rome, invented the Roman calendar around 753 B.C. It had six months with 30 days and four months with 31 days. The year began in March and ended in December. The calendar had a leap month once every few years to accommodate for the gap between the solar and lunar years. It was succeeded by the Julian calendar.

No January or February!
The most striking feature of the ancient Roman calendar was that there was no January

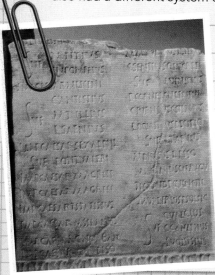

or February. The calendar had only 304 days and did not account for the remaining 61 days of January and February! Around 700 BCE, King Numa Pompilius reformed the calendar, introducing the months of January and February. This increased the year's length to 364 and 365 days.

FAST FACT . . .
The Greeks used the Golden Ratio to construct proportional rectangles, which they believed were the most accurate. Phidias, a Greek sculptor and mathematician, used it in many sculpture designs, such as the statue of the goddess Athena in Athens, the statue of Zeus in Olympiad, and the Parthenon.

FAST FACT . . .
The golden ratio is a special number that approximately equals to 1.618. In fact, the ancient Greeks saw this ratio as being so special that they gave it its own name and they called it "Phi."

17. THE GREGORIAN CALENDAR

The Gregorian calendar is a universally accepted calendar today. It was invented by Pope Gregory XIII in February, 1582. People set aside their traditional calendars and started following the Gregorian calendar. Today, almost every country and every person follows the Gregorian calendar.

Most of us are well-versed with the Gregorian calendar. It has 12 months of unequal lengths and is 365 and one quarter day long. The 12 months are January, February, March, April, May, June, July, August, September, October, November, and December. In a regular year, February has 28 days. April, June, September, and November are 30 days long while the remaining months are 31 days long.

The Leap Year
The leap year is a year in the Gregorian calendar that occurs once every four years and is

divisible by four. For example, the year 2012 was a leap year. The next leap year is 2016, and so on. In a leap year, the month of February has 29 days. The reason for this adjustment is that the solar year is 365 and one quarter days long. Every year is only 365 days long. Hence, every four years, the four quarter days are put together to make one full day, which is included in the month of February. This helps us ensure that the Gregorian calendar remains aligned with the equinoxes while also keeping in line with the solar year.

FAST FACT . . .

The sum of the total days in five consecutive months of the Gregorian calendar always equals to 153 and never exceeds it! Try doing this simple addition with any five different sets of months, excluding February.

18. THE ISLAMIC CALENDAR

The Islamic Calendar is a lunar calendar. It is based on the cycles of the moon. It is widely followed in most Islamic countries. Major Islamic festivals are based on this calendar. Apart from the Gregorian calendar, the Islamic calendar is probably the most widely followed calendar in modern times. It is followed by most countries in North Africa, the Middle East, and parts of Asia for religious purposes.

The Islamic calendar is also called the "Hijri" calendar. It sets the dates for all Islamic traditions and festivals. It is a lunar calendar consisting of 12 months in a year of 354 or 355 days. It runs concurrently with the Gregorian calendar in most Islamic countries.

622 A.D., was the first year in the Islamic calendar. This was when Prophet Muhammad emigrated from Mecca to Medina. This event is referred to as "Hijra." Each numbered year is designated using the letter H,

which is referred to as Hijra or AH which means "in the year of Hijra."

The Days of the Week

The Islamic calendar differs from the Gregorian calendar based on when a day begins. According to it, the first day of the week corresponds to Sunday in a planetary week. As opposed to the concept of a new day beginning at midnight according to the Gregorian calendar, a new day begins at sunset in this calendar. Every month in the Islamic calendar has some religious significance, with four months being highly sacred.

FAST FACT . . .

Though the Gregorian calendar is commonly used for recording dates and business purposes around the world, it is not the only calendar used in modern times. There are five other regular and commonly used calendars which are the Hebrew Calendar, the Islamic Calendar, the Persian Calendar, the Ethiopian Calendar, and the Balinese Pawukon.

19. THE HINDU CALENDAR

Indians have been pioneers in the field of mathematics since ancient times. Possessing detailed knowledge about different facets of mathematics way before many other civilizations, they were able to come up with calendars based on lunar and solar years. There were numerous traditional calendars that were also followed, but the Hindu calendar is found to be the most accurate of them all.

The Hindu calendar is also referred to as the Indian National Calendar. It is a lunar-solar calendar that considers the cycles of the moon as well as the Earth's revolution around the Sun. The Indian National calendar starts on March 22 of the Gregorian calendar and March 21 in every leap year. 78 A.D. is considered as the first day of the Hindu calendar. Hence, as per the Hindu calendar, the year 2013-14 corresponds to the year 1934-35 as per the Hindu calendar.

Even though the Hindu calendar is only followed parallel to the Gregorian calendar, it can safely be said that the Hindu calendar is among the most widely followed calendars in the world. All important Hindu festivals like Holi and Diwali are based on it. The Hindu Calendar starts with "Chaitra," the first month, which corresponds to March, while "Phalguna" is the last month that corresponds to February in the Gregorian calendar. Each month has either 30 or 31 days. The entire year is 365 days long.

It has not undergone too many changes since ancient times and is quite accurate and in sync with the equinoxes as well.

The Hindu calendar was remarkably shaped and reformed by famous Indian astronomers like Aryabhatta, Varahamihira, and Bhaskara II.

Statue of Aryabhatta

FAST FACT . . .

The dates of most Indian festivals change from year to year and are based on the Hindu calendar. There are so many festivals in India that it would be hard to keep a track of them without the Hindu calendar.

20. EGYPTIAN CALENDAR

Calendars have always been based on the motion of the Sun, moon, planetary bodies, stars, and different theories. Even though the ancient Egyptian calendar is about 5000 years old, it is strikingly similar to the calendar we use today.

During its initial stages, the Egyptian calendar followed the lunar cycle, which had 12 months. The Egyptians divided these 12 months into three seasons of four months each. The calendar, due to numerous reasons, was quite complicated and not accurate enough. Hence, it was replaced in the course of time.

Influence of the Nile

The calendar was based on the rising and falling phases of the great river Nile that flows

through Egypt. The Nile flooded around June every year. But the exact timing was very inaccurate and could vary up to an interval of 80 days. The Egyptians roughly approximated that the rising of the Nile roughly coincided with the heliacal rising of the brightest star in the sky, Sirius. Hence, the cycle of its reappearance became the basis for the Egyptian calendar.

The Three Seasons
The three seasons, according to the ancient Egyptian calendar were "Akhet," which was when the Nile flooded, "Proyet," which was when the Nile receded, and "Shumo," which was summertime for the Egyptians.

FAST FACT . . .
Ancient Egyptian festivals, such as the Opet festival and the festival of the Valley, were all based around the Nile and its nature.

FAST FACT . . .
Many different calendars have been created till the 20th century, but were not as accurate as the Egyptian one. Can you imagine how advanced the Egyptians were to get it right over 5000 years ago?

21. MAGIC MAYAN CALENDAR

The Mayans were known to be great mathematicians. They had a good understanding of astronomy as well. Their calendar systems were very different from other ancient calendars. Though the knowledge of the Mayan calendar was destroyed with the Spanish conquest, archeologists have been able to reconstruct parts of it piece by piece since the 1990s.

The Mayan calendar stated that the world would end in December 2012. The news of this dreaded apocalypse spread all over the world, and people waited to see if they would survive this tragedy. They heaved a sigh of relief when this prediction turned out to be incorrect!

The Three Mayan Calendars
One of the defining features of the three calendars that the Mayans followed was the fact that they had nothing to do with the motion of the planets, moon, Sun, or any other star. The Mayans knew about planetary motion and were fully aware of the solar year, but did not consider it essential to configure their ancient calendars around it.

There were three separate calendars that they followed. The "Long Count" calendar

FAST FACT . . .

The word "calendar" comes from the Latin word "Kalendae," meaning the first day of the month.

The "Tzolkin" calendar was used for all ceremonial purposes and had 260 days divided into 20 equal periods of 13 days.

FAST FACT . . .

Mayan monuments, such as pyramids, were built to tell time based on the movement of sunlight. Ruined cities such as Chichen Itza and Palenque still hold exquisite ruins of such remarkable monuments. They served as giant sundial!

was used to define a millennium (thousand years). The "Civil Calendar" was called the "Haab," with 360 days divided into 18 equal periods of 20 days. To stay in line with the solar year, five days were added at the end of each year.

22. TIME TALES

It is not possible to accurately determine when people first started keeping track of time. However, they found one way or another to do so. Some of the earliest devices for measuring time have been adapted into complex time-keeping devices like atomic clocks that we use today.

Time is an extremely important factor for us today. Most of the ancient methods of keeping time were based on the motion of celestial bodies like the Sun, moon, stars, and other celestial objects.

Initially, time was kept based on natural observations of day and night. Man would have developed an understanding of seasons and the length of the day and night, among other things. One fine day, early man devised an easy method of keeping track of time.

He decided to wedge a stick into the ground and observe its shadow's changing position during different parts of the day. The shadow's position would change exactly the way a clock hand moves in a circle, making this wedged stick the first man-made clock.

The part of the stick that cast the shadow came to be known as the "gnomon." This became the most important component of a sundial, which was an early device used to measure time. It is believed that the sundial was invented by the Egyptians.

FAST FACT . . .

In 1836, a young gentleman named John Bellville decided to sell time. He set his pocket watch at the Greenwich Observatory where he worked. He would sell the precise time to his clients in the city every morning. This became his family's business all the way up to 1940!

FAST FACT . . .

Even though September is the ninth month of the year in the Gregorian calendar, the word "September" is derived from the word "septa," meaning seven! This is because there were 10 months in the original calendar from which the Gregorian calendar was derived, and September was the seventh month back then.

23. SUNDIALS

Sundials are the most primitive devices that were used to keep track of time. Invented by the Egyptians, several other civilizations such as the Mayans also worked on its development, coming up with various different versions of it.

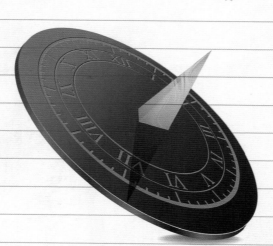

The earliest portable sundial to be found is the Egyptian shadow clock. It became popular around 1500 B.C. It was basically a T-shaped or L-shaped device. Its end bar was raised to cast a shadow based on the movement of the Sun during the morning hours. They were then turned around in the afternoon to keep track of time from afternoon to evening. While the Egyptian shadow clock is the earliest time keeping device to be discovered, other civilizations like the Babylonians, Mayans, Indians, Greeks, and Chinese also came up with different versions of clocks around the same time.

Ancient civilization did not know that Earth revolves around the Sun in an elliptical orbit. They considered the orbit to be circular. Due to this incorrect assumption, when the Sun was closer to Earth, its shadow would seem to move faster around the sundial as compared to when it was farther away. Hence, the sundial did not show time uniformly through the year. One more factor that caused problems in measuring time with a sundial was the assumption that Earth's axis was vertical, which isn't true. Earth's axis is tilted. This caused some mistakes in maintaining the accuracy of time keeping, creating a difference of around 15 minutes. This might not seem like too much, but has an impact in the long run.

FAST FACT . . .

Sweden took a lot of time to catch up with the Gregorian calendar, as their calendar was quite different. They included 30 days in every month of February from 1700 to 1740 to catch up with the Gregorian calendar. As a result, none of their dates matched with the dates in any other country during that period!

24. DEVELOPED DIALS

The transition from sundials to clocks was quite a monumental step in the history of mankind. Man no longer felt the need to depend on the movement of the Sun in order to keep track of time. From the earliest clocks, which did not have minute or second hands, to modern time-telling devices, there has been a huge transformation.

With the decline of the sundial came the popularity of the hour-glass and the water clock. Hour- glasses, in which sand flowed from one glass bulb to another, and water clocks, which used dripping water to keep track of time, started gaining popularity.

It was around 1300 that mechanical clocks were first introduced. They initially used weights and springs to assist movement and show time. Unlike our modern day clocks, the earliest mechanical clocks had no face and no minute or second hands. Instead, they had a bell that rang at the end of every hour. From there on, as man developed different machines and devices, such as the coiled spring, clocks continued to grow more sophisticated. Mathematician and scientist, Christian Huygens, came up with the legendary pendulum clock in 1656. It used weights and a swinging pendulum. This kind of clock is popularly referred to as the "grandfather's clock." Some of us may

2009
CHRISTIAN HUYGENS

RWANDA

have seen huge clocks as big as cupboards that serve as decorative pieces today. These pendulum clocks had an accuracy close to within a minute and the ones with bigger pendulums were even more accurate. The 20th century has also seen the development of state-of-the-art atomic clocks as advancements in this field are being made on a daily basis.

FAST FACT . . .

The smallest unit of time is known as "Planck time." It is much smaller than a nanosecond, which is one billionth of a second!

CALCULUS

PROBABILITY

MENSURATION

SHAPE

MEASUREMENT

PI

ARITHMETIC

ALGEBRA

TRIGONOMETRY

BRANCHES OF MATH

FORMULAS

GEOMETRY

25. ALGEBRA - THE X FACTOR

Most of us are not huge fans of Algebra. However, in course of time we understand that algebra is a branch of mathematics that is not very different from arithmetic. A lot of developments in the modern world would have been impossible in the absence of Algebra.

$$\sqrt{xy^2} = z$$

$$\frac{2}{3}x^2 - \sqrt{x}$$

$$x^2 - 3^2 - 4^2 = 0$$

$$\frac{3}{\sqrt{x}} = 0$$

$$x = y - \frac{b}{3a}$$

$$\frac{x^2 + y^2}{a^2} + \frac{z^2}{b^2} = 1$$

$$(a+b)^2 = a^2 + 2ab + b^2$$

$$x = \frac{-b \pm \sqrt{b^2 - 4ac}}{2a}$$

$$y^3 + py + q = 0$$

$$1 + 1 = 2$$

$$x = \sqrt{\frac{b^2}{c} + c - \frac{b}{2}}$$

$$a^2 - b^2 = (a-b)(a+b)$$

$$g(x) = \sqrt{x(x-a)(x-b)}$$

$$x^3 + x = c$$

Algebra is a branch of mathematics which makes use of symbols like "α" (alpha) and letters like "x" to represent values that are unknown or are variable in nature. The goal of algebra is to find the value of these unknown variables. As such, algebra is applied in any field that needs to find the value of unknown quantities or to define the limits of certain variables. Algebra and its components could be best understood with an example. Let's say you have two movie tickets and you are going with your best friend. Suddenly, two more friends also want to join you, and you can't turn them down. How many more tickets will you have to buy now? Let's say the extra number of tickets to be bought is "x." We need 4 tickets in all, and we have only 2 at the moment. So, the sum of "x" and "2" should be equal to "4" or "x + 2 = 4." This means that — "x = 4 – 2 = 2." Thus, the number of extra tickets that need to be bought for all of you to attend the movie together is 2. That's algebra!

FAST FACT . . .

The word Algebra is derived from the title of a book written by famous Arab mathematician Al-Khwarizmi. It is called "Al-jabr wa'l Muqbalah'I." The title means "restored and balanced," which is the way equations are dealt with in algebra.

FAST FACT . . .

The most common methodology used to refer to unknown quantities is to denote them by making use of the letter "x." The letters that are commonly used after "x" are "y" and "z."

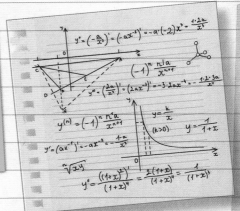

26. TRIGONOMETRY

Another important and interesting branch of mathematics is trigonometry. Known as the mathematics of triangles, trigonometry has been developed since early times by Indian, Greek, and Egyptian mathematicians. Complex structures like the Pyramids built thousands of years ago can be credited to trigonometry.

This intriguing branch of mathematics deals with the angles and sides of a triangle and, in most cases, those of a right-angled triangle. This is a triangle in which one angle is 90° or perfectly vertical with respect to the horizontal surface.

Trigonometry is a subject filled with formulae. Sine, Cosine, Tangent, Cosecant, Secant, and Cotangent are six major functions of this subject. These six functions help calculate the area of a surface by splitting it into a triangular structure, for example, a circle.

Sin Function: Sin(θ) = Opposite / Hypotenuse	
Cosine Function:	**cos(θ) = Adjacent / Hypotenuse**
Tangent Function:	**tan(θ) = Opposite / Adjacent**
Cosecant Function:	**csc(θ) = Hypotenuse / Opposite**
Secant Function:	**sec(θ) = Hypotenuse / Adjacent**
Cotangent Function:	**cot(θ) = Adjacent / Opposite**

$$\frac{a}{\sin\alpha} = \frac{b}{\sin\beta} = \frac{c}{\sin\gamma} = 2R$$

$$2\sin^2\alpha = 1 - \cos 2\alpha$$

$$\cos^2\alpha - \sin^2\alpha$$

$$\cos 2\alpha = 2\cos^2\alpha - 1$$

$$tg(\alpha - \beta) = \frac{tg\alpha - tg\beta}{1 + tg\alpha\, tg\beta}$$

$$\log_a b^r = r\log_a b$$

$$ctg^2\alpha + 1 = \frac{1}{\sin^2\alpha} = cosec^2\alpha$$

$$\log_b c = \frac{\log_c c}{\log_c b}$$

$$a^{\log_b c} = c^{\log_b a}$$

$$\cos\alpha - \cos\beta =$$

$$\sin\alpha - \sin\beta = 2\sin\frac{\alpha-\beta}{2}\cos\frac{\alpha+\beta}{2}$$

Trigonometry is vital in fields like architecture, where it is used to build roof slopes, buildings, towers, etc. It is also used in astronomy, rocket science, navigation at sea, and for many other purposes, including mountain climbing!

FAST FACT . . .

Though the full name of this beautiful subject is mathematics, there is a lot of confusion over whether the short form is "math" or "maths." It is believed that "math" is grammatically correct as mathematics is a singular noun. So "math" as a singular noun is correct, whereas "maths" is an incorrect term that is often used to refer to mathematics!

27. GEOMETRY-SHAPING IT UP

As a branch of mathematics, geometry is probably one that is most commonly applied to every field of life. Geometry is a branch that can easily be seen all around us! Greek mathematician Thales of Miletus first set the basic rules and defined the branch of geometry.

Geometry, as a branch of mathematics, has undergone a lot of development. The number of sub-branches in geometry grows frequently. In the earliest times, it was considered to be a part of Quadrivium, along with astronomy by the Greeks. Quadrivium was a subset of one of the seven liberal arts considered essential for a free citizen to master.

Many great mathematicians from the ancient and medieval times, like Euclid, Euler, Archimedes, and Gauss, have made important contributions to geometry. This has resulted

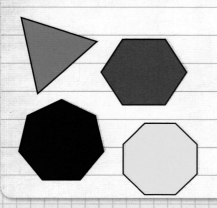

in its wide scale development. In fact, mathematicians like Euclid and Gauss have completely different sub branches of geometry named after them.

As time passed, newer shapes were discovered and developed, such as pentagons (five sides), octagons (eight sided), and dodecagons (twelve sided), among several others. Co-ordinate geometry, which deals with the position of objects in space, has also undergone widespread development. Today, it is possible to accurately calculate the position of stars that are millions of miles away! Since geometry has so many applications, it would be difficult to define a mere few. It would be safe to say that geometry is a part of every thing you see from the day you were born!

FAST FACT . . .
After arithmetic, geometry is the second oldest field of mathematics. It Is used and studied since the ancient times. Civilizations, like those of the Egyptians and Babylonians, used it to make marvelous structures that would have been impossible without the knowledge of it.

FAST FACT . . .
Pi (π) is a symbol that stands for the value of 3.14 or 22/7. It is used for all calculations related to a circle.

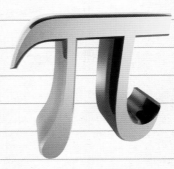

28. ARITHMETIC

Arithmetic is the first branch of mathematics that ever developed. Subconsciously, human beings have been using arithmetic even before they realized, developed, and understood the concept of mathematics. The most elementary branch of mathematics, arithmetic is the branch through which we are introduced to mathematics. It stays with us until the rest of our lives!

Arithmetic is the name given to a branch of mathematics that deals with the elementary operations of addition, subtraction, multiplication, and division. There are several approaches to arithmetic, which have been developed by ancient civilizations. Some of them include Vedic Math and Abacus Math. More than a field of study, it is a skill that we ought to master to make our daily lives a lot easier!
For starters, you wouldn't have been able to count your pocket money without arithmetics.
You could also bid farewell

FAST FACT . . .

Every year, March 14 is celebrated as World Math Day across the world to celebrate the beautiful subject of mathematics.

to all your favorite sports like basketball, baseball, and football, because there would have been no way to keep track of the score in these games. There would have been no way to buy or sell anything as we would have no method of calculating the money owned or owed.

Apart from its basic application, arithmetic has been used for some extremely complex application as well! Islamic scholars taught the applications of rulings related to Zakat and Irth. It is also used in fields like taxation, trading, and every possible field of business.

29. CREATIVE CALCULUS

Calculus, along with geometry and arithmetic, forms the core of mathematics. Each of these fields is extremely different in approach and purpose, but complement each other at the same time. Calculus also happens to be a relatively new field in mathematics as compared to geometry and arithmetic. Leibnitz and Isaac Newton can be called the inventors of calculus. Even though it is a branch of mathematics that was introduced much later, it is of great significance in numerous fields.

Calculus can be defined, in simple words, as the branch of mathematics that deals with change. It is a branch that has actually been derived from geometry and arithmetic. A lot of its ideas were developed by ancient civilizations like those of the Indians, Babylonians, and Persians. But it was only in medieval Europe that calculus first gained any kind of importance. It was the work of Leibnitz and Isaac Newton that led to several proofs and the foundation for calculus.

Calculus has two broad divisions; differential and

integral calculus. Differential calculus deals with finding out the rate of change in certain quantities and with the slopes of curves. Integral calculus deals with the build up or accumulation of quantities and the areas under various curves. One of the major applications of calculus is in finding the slope of a curve. While finding out the slope of a line is relatively easier, trying to compute the slope of a curve is a different matter altogether. Other important applications include finding areas of slopes, visualizing graphs, and finding optimum values for various functions that are extremely helpful in various fields of science and architecture.

FAST FACT . . .

An interesting tool used in geometry is the "tomahawk," which is used for angle trisection. Its boundaries include a semicircle and two line segments. Since it is commonly used by shoemakers as well, it is also referred to as the "shoe-maker's knife."

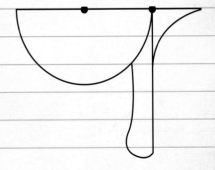

30. PREDICTION & PROBABILITY

One of the most interesting and logical branches of mathematics is probability. Developed in medieval times by mathematicians like Freidrich Gauss and Christen Huygens, probability has actually led to a mathematical understanding in the world of betting. Odds on a certain player or team winning are placed based on answers received through the mathematical branch of probability.

Probability is the field of mathematics that deals with the study of the possibility of certain outcomes. It can be best understood with an example. Let us consider a coin that you wish to throw into a pool. There are two ways in which it lands. It will land on its head or its tail.

There are two possible outcomes. As we know, the chances for both are equal. If we generalize this, we can say that the probability of any event occurring is equal to the ratio of the number of ways in which it can occur (in this case, only one) to the total number of possible outcomes (in this case, two). Therefore, probability is unlike most other branches of mathematics. It only gives you the possibility of a certain event occurring, and does not prove in any way that the event is going to occur. It is inaccurate and is therefore used in a scarce manner, only for particular fields.

FAST FACT . . .

If you want to get a certain 10 digit number as your cell phone number and you are choosing it randomly from the entire set of numbers, probability states that there is only one in a million chance that you will actually get it.

31. THE MATRIX

A "matrix" or "matrices" are rectangular arrays of numbers where numbers are arranged in rows and columns. With numerous applications in the field of optics, geometry, electronics, etc., matrices have assumed immense importance due to the simple fact that they make solving complex equations or difficult calculations a lot easier.

Even though calculators are used for similar applications as matrices, the latter still has an important role to play in the role of software development, programming, and various other fields. Consider an array that consists of four numbers, two in each row and two in each column. A box of this sort is called a matrix.

A matrix can have any number of rows and columns, provided the total numbers in each row are equal and the total numbers in each column are also equal. Different elementary operations of arithmetic, such as addition,

m-by-n matrix

$a_{i,j}$ n columns **j changes**

m rows

i changes

$$
\begin{matrix}
a_{1,1} & a_{1,2} & a_{1,3} & \cdots \\
a_{2,1} & a_{2,2} & a_{2,3} & \cdots \\
a_{3,1} & a_{3,2} & a_{3,3} & \cdots \\
\vdots & \vdots & \vdots & \ddots
\end{matrix}
$$

subtraction, and multiplication, can be carried out on matrices. How to carry them out is something you will learn in higher classes.

Matrices have widespread applications in the fields of economics, analysis, and statistics. Various complex operations are carried out on matrices. Many fields of physics, especially optical physics, make use of matrices for complex computations. The method of receiving solutions using arrays is very common in computer programming. Matrices are also important in the fields of geometric optics and electronics.

$$\begin{bmatrix} 1 & 8 & 13 & 12 \\ 14 & 11 & 2 & 7 \\ 4 & 5 & 16 & 9 \\ 15 & 10 & 3 & 6 \end{bmatrix}$$

FAST FACT . . .

The Matrix trilogy is an interesting series of movies that showcases this branch of mathematics. The three movies are "The Matrix Revolution," "The Matrix Reloaded," and "Enter the Matrix."

32. MENSURATION

Mensuration is a field of mathematics that deals with measuring areas, volume, or lengths of different geometric shapes. Being of great importance in the field of construction and architecture, it is used to calculate the length, height, and width of objects required to achieve a certain area or volume. With the growth, development, and progress of geometry, mensuration is also progressing at a rapid pace.

Mensuration, just like geometry is branch of mathematics that deals with objects of different shapes and sizes. It goes in to the study of their areas, volumes, and lengths. How do you think the carpenter arrived at a conclusion to give a table its height and length? The answer to this question can be

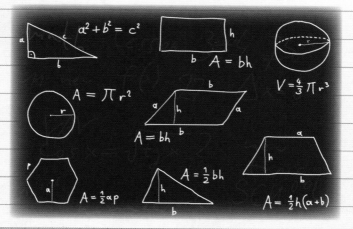

obtained from mensuration. The carpenter who made this rectangular or square object would have probably been told to follow a certain area and a certain height. He would then calculate the required length by using mensuration. This branch contains different formulae, which can be used to calculate the areas and volumes of different geometric shapes. For example, the area of a rectangle can be obtained by multiplying its length and its breadth (Area=length x breadth).

Similarly, there are different formulae for computing the areas of almost all geometric shapes, such as squares, triangles, pentagons, hexagons, circles, cylinders, etc. In its absence, we wouldn't be able to decide the height of a cupboard to fit into a particular room or the length of pipe needed to reach from one end of a garden to another.

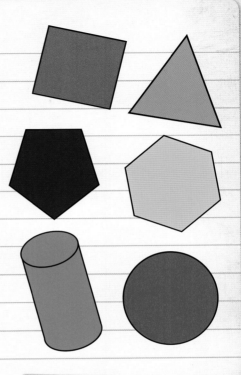

FAST FACT . . .
The word "hundred," used for the number 100, is actually derived from the word "hundrath" in Old Norse, which means 120 and not 100!

33. COMPLEX NUMBERS

Complex numbers are a topic that you will probably study in higher classes. However, their importance to mathematics, and to different applications in which they are used, is extremely significant. Once we learn about complex numbers, we will be introduced to a completely new field of mathematics involving "imaginary numbers."

For a very long time, complex numbers were unknown to the mathematical world. A complete branch of mathematics did not exist until then. Computation and calculations with numbers were limited to a particular type. It was only in the 1500s that Italian mathematician Gerolama Cardano introduced the world to complex numbers. He called a certain

set of numbers "fictitious." Today, they are referred to as "imaginary numbers." Complex numbers are of two types; real and imaginary. Real numbers are normal positive integers, fractions, and decimals that we see in normal mathematical calculations.

Let's take the example of 9. The square root of 9 is 3, and when 3 is multiplied by itself, it gives us 9. However, when we deal with the square roots of negative numbers, things are slightly different. The square root of a negative number cannot be obtained in a simple way as we obtain the square root of a positive number. The square root of a negative number is always an imaginary number. This forms the basis of complex numbers.

FAST FACT . . .

Can you try getting 1000 as the answer by making use of eight 8s and using the arithmetic operation of addition only? Give it a try. The trick lies in arranging 8 in a certain way to obtain different numbers before adding them. Here's the answer:
888+88+8+8+8 = 1000!

FIBONACCI

EUCLID

DESCARTES

LAGRANGE

GAUSS

RAMANUJAN

ARCHIMEDES

FIBONACCI

PYTHAGORAS

MATHEMATICIANS WHO CHANGED THE WORLD

LEIBNITZ

EULER

DESCARTES

34. EUCLID OF ALEXANDRIA

Euclid of Alexandria is among the greatest Greek mathematicians ever. He revolutionized the field of geometry. "Euclid's Elements" is often called the Bible of geometry. Though Euclid is known for his contributions to the field of geometry, it would be interesting to note that he contributed to almost all branches of mathematics known to us, including trigonometry and arithmetic.

EUCLIDES

thinker of his time. His audience comprised of several important people in the Greek society.

Euclid's Elements

In the book "Euclid's Elements," he compiled the works of his predecessors, such as Hippocrates of Chios, Aristotle, and Theudius, while coming up with his own axioms, notions, and rules for geometry and other fields of mathematics. Even though this book was inspired by the work of his predecessors, its contents were well and truly his effort and genius. He only used

Around 300 B.C., Euclid came up with several theorems and notions of Geometry, which continue to remain immensely relevant. Euclid is also believed to have been a very influential

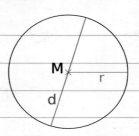

Some of the important notions he came up with include –

- Two points can be joined by a single straight line.
- A straight line segment can be prolonged infinitely.
- A circle can be constructed if its center point and radius are known.
- The whole is always greater than the part.

some of the teachings of his predecessors to come up with those of his own and also refined the past ones. Euclid's works in geometry resulted in the construction of the five regular solids, which are the cube, tetrahedron, iso-octahedron, do-decahedron, and the tetrahedron. These are called Platonic Solids.

35. LEIBNITZ OF LEIPZIG

Leibnitz, with Sir Isaac Newton, is considered to be the inventor of modern calculus. A lot of his theorems form the basis for calculus, one of the most important branches of mathematics. He had a tough childhood, but having been one of the most intelligent people ever, he was able to overcome all obstacles and redefine philosophy and mathematics.

By the age of 20, Gottfried Wilhelm Leibnitz mastered teachings of important textbooks of mathematics, law, theology, and philosophy. Talk about being smart! He was so smart that the envious citizens of Leipzig refused him a doctorate, which forced him to migrate to Nuremburg.

Contribution to Mathematics

Leibnitz came up with most of his theorems and wrote most of his articles while serving as a librarian in Hannover. He worked in close association with mathematicians like Isaac Newton and Christen

2012

Huygens to further develop the field of geometry. However, he is best remembered for the invention of infinitesimal calculus. Sir Isaac Newton and Leibnitz worked in close association to co-invent calculus. Some of the most important signs, such as those of differentiation and integration, have been invented by Leibnitz. He made significant contributions towards the development of the calculator, and also helped develop binary language. If there was a poll to judge the smartest man ever, he would have probably finished a close second to Albert Einstein.

36. PYTHAGORAS

Pythagoras of Samos is widely considered as the first great mathematician. His disciples and students, who took his theorems, research, and teachings forward, were called Pythagoreans. They are considered to be the first ones to take up mathematics seriously. A multifaceted man, he was also known to have been a great philosopher.

His mathematical concepts and theorems are commonly used by us even today. Pythagoras lived between 570 B.C. and 495 B.C. in Greece. Apart from being a great mathematician himself, his philosophical teachings influenced many philosophers, who called themselves the "Pythagoreans."

The Pythagoras' Theorem
Pythagoras was the first mathematician to prove that the sum of the angles of a triangle is equal to two right angles. He also revolutionized and developed the field of geometry by finding methods to solve several equations using

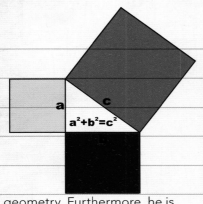

a c
$a^2+b^2=c^2$

geometry. Furthermore, he is
believed to have been the first
person to construct regular
solids like the cube, tetrahedron
(four sided), and octahedron
(eight sided). He also stated that
the Earth was a sphere and he
believed it was located in the
center of the universe.

But the theorem that has
immortalized his name is
the "Pythagoras Theorem."
According to this theorem, the
square on the length of the
hypotenuse (longest side of a
right-angled triangle) is equal
to the sum of the square of the
lengths of the other two sides
of the triangle. As long as right
angled triangles exist, he will
never be forgotten!

37. RENE DESCARTES

Having been the first person to link algebra and geometry, Rene Descartes and his principles helped develop a branch of mathematics that deals with the position of objects in a particular space or environment. Being among the first French philosophers and mathematicians with great influence, Rene Descartes inspired several mathematicians to further develop his teachings.

Though Rene Descartes holds a very important place in the world of mathematics, he is also considered to be the "father of modern philosophy." Descartes' writings have inspired Western philosophy over and above everything else in its field. Born in La Haye (which is now called Descartes in his honor) in France, Descartes spent a major portion of his life in the Dutch Republic.

Contribution to Mathematics

"Regulae" or "Rules for the Direction of Mind" was his first book, in which he discussed various methods. From then on, Descartes wrote several different books related to mathematics and philosophy. "Discourse on Method, Optics, Geometry, and Meteorology" was among the main and most popular books of Descartes. In this book, he blends the teachings of algebra and geometry to invent the field of Cartesian geometry. Thanks to this invention, the position of any object in a three dimensional (3D) space can be identified if other information is known.

FAST FACT . . .

British philosopher Bertrand Russell had a different take on mathematics. He once said, "Mathematics is the subject in which we neither know what we are talking about nor what we are saying is true."

His main contribution to mathematics was coming up with a method for many different axioms and notions of mathematicians of the past, like Euclid and Euler. He believed that there was a proof to everything and worked hard to find a lot of them.

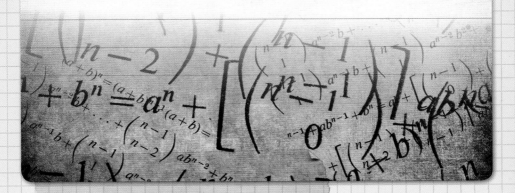

38. CARL FREIDRICH GAUSS

Carl Freidrich Gauss is rightly called "The Prince of Mathematics." He came up with amazing mathematical discoveries and theorems at a young age when people like us are still learning the basics of mathematics! He also wrote one of the greatest mathematics books when he was a teenager. Through his lifetime, he redefined the field of mathematics and physics.

Carl Freidrich Gauss was a child prodigy. Born in Brunswick, Germany, the teachers at his primary school realized very early that he was a genius. At the young age of seven, he was able to add up all numbers from 1 to 100 in just a few seconds using a smart trick. He realized that there were 50 pairs of numbers from 1 to 100, each adding up to 101 (1+100, 2+99, and so on). He simply multiplied 101 by 50 to get the answer, which is 5050. He wrote "Disquisition's Arithmeticae" while he was still a teenager.

That's one amazing feat for a teenager, as this book is one of the greatest books on mathematics ever written!

FAST FACT . . .

Famous mathematician Simeon Poisson was so obsessed with mathematics and in love with it to such a great extent that he once said, "Life is good for only two things, discovering mathematics and teaching mathematics."

Major Contributions to Mathematics

Once he graduated from university, he made research in mathematics his full time job. While coming up with new proofs, theorems, and corollaries for different fields of mathematics, his major contribution to it was the number theory. He developed the concept of prime numbers. He also successfully proved the fundamental theorem of algebra, something that several mathematicians before him had tried but failed to achieve.

39. LEONHARD EULER

The great Leonhard Euler is widely regarded as the "King of Mathematics." According to numerous polls, he is regarded as the greatest mathematician ever. His impact on the field of mathematics is such that several intellects in this field born centuries after him have been unable to come up with contributions like his or reach the level that he did with the minimal resources that he possessed. His impact can be seen in every field of mathematics.

Born on April 15, 1707, Swiss mathematician Euler taught at the University of St. Petersburg along with Johann Bernoulli's son before traveling to different parts of Europe, including Berlin and other parts of Russia. Euler was known to be quite eccentric and believed that everything could be done theoretically. He often forgot to take important practical aspects into consideration. He was quite a simple man who was extremely passionate about his work. He was often quite misunderstood.

Euler's Contributions to Mathematics

It is believed that all mathematical formulae are named after the person who discovered them.

Charles Darwin

This happened after Euler's death in 1783, otherwise it would be very confusing to have every formula named after Euler! Some say that he is as smart as Einstein. He came up with Euler's gravitational constant, the notation "e," as the base of the natural logarithm, the notation "i" for complex numbers, the Greek letter "sigma" used for summations, and even the symbol for "pi!" He also developed calculus, topology, the number theory, and solved complex problems never solved before.

40. ALAN TURING

Alan Turing is one of the greatest minds of the 20th century. This British mathematician, logician, and computer scientist contributed to victory of the Allied Powers, including the United Kingdom over the Nazis of Germany and the other Axis Powers during World War II. He also revolutionized the field of computer science and is partly responsible for the way we see computers today.

One of the major challenges for both warring factions during World War II was to decipher and crack the coded messages of the enemies.

It was a common trend for armies to send messages from one check post to another in a certain coded language only understood by them. If their messages were intercepted, the enemy would be unable to read them. Alan Turing belonged to the Government Code and Cypher School, which was Britain's code breaking center.

Using his in-depth knowledge of mathematical logic and reasoning, he cracked several codes of this type and helped Allied Armies as well as British Armies intercept and decipher important messages of the Nazi

Army during the war.
He is considered the best code breaker ever, coming up with new and inventive ways to crack several difficult codes.

Contributions to Mathematics
After the war, Alan Turing furthered his studies in the field of mathematical computation. He wanted to develop an electronic machine capable of mathematical computation. This machine is what we popularly refer to as the computer today! His series of papers on Artificial Intelligence and other areas of mathematical computation are of immense importance even today. Furthermore, he developed the famous Turing test, which is still used to evaluate the intelligence and effectiveness of computers.
He was extremely intelligent and a master in the game of chess. A lot of his initial knowledge about the game was used to develop artificial intelligence in computers.
He died mysteriously of cyanide poisoning in 1954.

41. PAUL ERDOS

Like Alan Turing, Paul Erdos is one of the most influential mathematicians of the 20th century. A phenomenal individual who made mathematics his life, he traveled all around the world, collaborating with different mathematicians and making contributions to different branches of mathematics. There was often a waiting list of mathematicians waiting to collaborate with him.

Paul Erdos was a Hungarian mathematician. He was born in 1913. Paul Erdos spent most of his time reading the mathematics books that belonged to his parents. At the age of three, he could multiply three digit numbers mentally with ease, when most of us are still learning single digit numbers! He discovered the magic of negative numbers at the age of four! He said that he considered numbers to be his best friend and fell in love with them.

Contribution to Mathematics

Erdos believed that God was the supreme mathematician. He had an extreme liking for prime numbers (3, 5, 7, 11...) and came up with proofs for many theorems related to them. After finishing his doctorate, he traveled around the world, coming up with various research papers and theories. Erdos developed interesting theorems in number theory, geometry, and trigonometry.

He loved working with other people and lived with the mantra, "another roof, another proof!" He often went uninvited to the homes of great mathematicians and spent months working on complex theorems and proofs with them.

FAST FACT . . .

The number of mathematicians wishing to collaborate with Paul Erdos was so huge that he introduced a number system. The closer your number was to 1, the closer it meant you were to Paul Erdos. It is believed that people had numbers running into thousands! Such was his popularity in mathematical circles.

He was probably the greatest student of mathematics. He traveled to over 22 countries, working on mathematical proofs and theorems.

42. BERNHARD RIEMANN

Bernhard Riemann was among the most brilliant mathematicians of the 19th century. His contributions to geometry are unparalleled. He also made various contributions to other fields like the number theory and differential calculus.

Apart from these, there is one unanswered question posed by him which was the cause of sleepless nights for many mathematicians! In his short life span of 40 years, Bernhard Riemann wrote his name in the history of mathematics. A German mathematician, he was born into a very poor family with limited resources in 1826. Riemann was a shy and timid kid who was scared of speaking up in public. However, his mathematics skills were exceptional and he had very good calculation abilities at a very early age.

His Million Dollar Question!

Riemann made his largest contributions to the field of geometry. There are various things in this branch of mathematics that have been named after him. These include Riemannian Geometry, Riemannian Surfaces, Riemannian Integrals, etc.

Though he came to be known for his numerous contributions to other fields of mathematics, what he is most widely remembered for and often infamous for is the Riemannian Hypothesis. It is an extremely complex mathematical problem that provides valuable insights into the world of prime numbers, and its solution remains unknown even today! A math institute has offered a million dollars to anybody who can correctly solve this problem as it is believed that it will lead to the development of a completely new field of mathematics.

FAST FACT . . .

If Riemann's million dollar question is ever answered, it could lead to the complete failure of a lot of present day security systems, password protection methods, and encryption codes. It is believed that it will result in mathematics getting redefined! A lot of people hope that this is one mathematical problem for which a solution is never found!

$$|\psi(t)| \leq \sum_{r=0}^{s} |c_r| t^r$$

$$\leq \frac{t^{p-1}}{(p-1)!} f((t+1)($$

$$\to 0, \text{ an}$$

43. FIBONACCI

Popularly referred to as Leonardo Fibonacci, he was a genius mathematician in the Middle Ages. He was a blessed mathematician who got direct access to both European as well as Arabic mathematics. He learnt from mathematical scholars of both regions, who had slightly different perspectives towards mathematics. He blended them together beautifully.

Born in Italy in 1170, Leonardo Fibonacci was deeply inspired by the teachings of Arab mathematicians. He realized how the Arabic numerals, which were actually the Hindu-Arabic numerals, were a lot more effective and easy to use as compared to Roman numerals. His biggest contribution to the world of mathematics was acquainting the European world with these numerals, which then went in to become a mainstay in Europe and are still used for listing purposes. It was through his book "Liber Abaci," written in 1202, that he was able to do this.

Another great contribution to mathematics made by him was the famous "Fibonacci Sequence." It is simply a series of numbers in which the next digit is the sum of the two digits

FAST FACT . . .

The number 8 is the largest cube number in the Fibonnaci series. There is no cube number beyond 8 in it. A cube number is the value of a number raised to 3. E.g. $2^3 = 8$.

FAST FACT . . .
144 is the largest square number in the Fibonacci sequence. 144 is the square of 12.

FAST FACT . . .
Dan Brown, the author of books like "The Da Vinci Code" and "Angels and Demons," has a very special liking for the Fibonacci Sequence. They play a very important role in solving the mysteries in these books.

before it, with the first two digits in the series being 0 and 1. The series is never ending. The series goes as follows – 0, 1, 1 (0+1), 2 (1+1), 3, 5, 8, 13, and so on. He also authored several important books on mathematics, apart from coming up with a variety of number sequences.

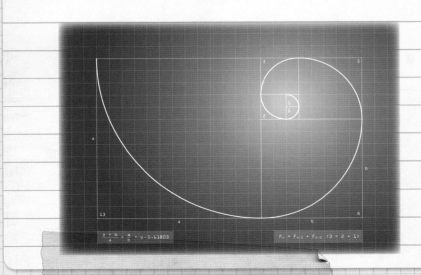

44. ARCHIMEDES

Born in Ancient Greece, Archimedes was a legend during his period. Multifaceted and obsessed with mathematics and creation, he devoted his life to research and the study of mathematics and physics. His contributions to mathematics are endless, and he also has several other inventions to his credit. He is one name that you are sure to read a lot more as you move to higher classes.

FAST FACT . . .

The Gold Crown
Archimedes was once asked to determine the purity of a gold crown that had been made for King Hierro. While doing this, Archimedes found out the density of gold and also the method to find out the volume of irregular objects. I guess we should also thank King Hierro!

Archimedes of Syracuse was a great mathematician, physicist, inventor, engineer, and astronomer. The trio – Sir Isaac Newton, Carl Freidrich Gauss, and Archimedes – are often considered the greatest mathematicians of all time. Around 500 A.D., when other great Roman mathematicians began researching his work, they realized that he had made massive contributions to the field of mathematics. Archimedes was obsessed with geometry. He determined a very accurate value of pi, centuries before anybody else did so. Using this value, he calculated the volume of a sphere. He also set the foundation for integral calculus, which was only developed by Sir Isaac Newton and Leibnitz more than 1500 years later. He could sum up an infinite series of numbers, and come up with the "Powers of Ten" counting method. He came up with the formula to compute the area under curves like parabola. The word "eureka," meaning "I have found it," was made famous by him!

FAST FACT . . .
Using his deep knowledge of mathematics and physics, Archimedes designed a weapon called the "ship shaker," which could make ships lose their balance. He did this to protect his home city of Syracuse.

The Archimedes screw, which helped farmers irrigate land.

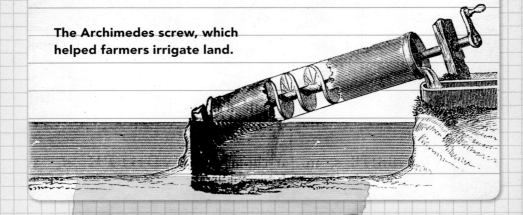

45. BRAHMAGUPTA

India had a rich tradition of mathematics since the ancient times. Many discoveries made by the European world were first made in India, centuries before the Europeans discovered them. Mathematics and science were a way of life. Indian books, like the Vedas, have extremely detailed proofs, theorems, and other important theories related to mathematics. Among the greatest mathematicians of ancient India was Brahmagupta. Born in 597, he was one of the greatest mathematicians the world has seen.

The number of theorems and methods were so many, that hundreds of mathematicians had to work for hundreds of years trying to prove them. Brahmagupta contributed greatly to number sequencing and the number theory as well. He is most remembered for providing the rules and a basis for the use of the number "zero." It can be said that he introduced the world of mathematics to "zero," which revolutionized the field of mathematics. In the field of algebra, Brahmagupta was a pioneer solving linear equations, quadratic equations, simultaneous equations, and difficult and indeterminate equations. He came up with a series for the sum of the cubes and squares of the first integers, and gave a formula for the entire sum, which is used even today.

He also came up with a decently accurate approximation for pi ,used for finding the area and volume of circles. He also contributed to trigonometry. Many mathematical formulae would be named after him if he received credit for each of them!

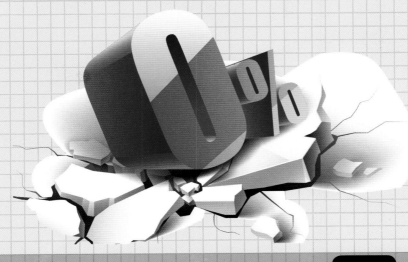

46. LAGRANGE

Lagrange was a gifted mathematician from the medieval period. He started contributing to the field of mathematics from a very young age. His work in the field of calculus has immortalized him. Unfortunately, he spent much of his early life working alone on complex mathematical theorems. He did not have direct access to some of the greatest mathematicians of the time, which is believed to have hindered his work.

Born in Turin, Italy, in 1736, Lagrange spent most of his life in France until his death in 1813. There is a lot of confusion over whether he was French or Italian, and there has been a great debate between these two countries, who want to prove that this great mathematician was one of their own!

Lagrange had humble beginnings. He did not receive formal education. His father served the king of Sardinia in a position of importance.

FAST FACT . . .

A well-known mathematician by the name of Johann von Neumann believed that mathematics could only be mastered with practice. As we get more and more exposed to numbers and the branches of mathematics, we further get used to them. He once said, "In mathematics, you don't understand things. You get used to them."

However, his father's addiction to gambling proved to be his undoing, and he lost a lot of money. His father always wanted Lagrange to be a lawyer and Lagrange willingly went to the University of Turin for this purpose. But his natural talent in mathematics took over and he decided to devote his life to it.

Contribution to Mathematics

Lagrange once said, "If I were rich, I wouldn't have devoted my life to mathematics." It was his humble beginnings that gave him exposure to the world of mathematics and his interest in it kept growing.

Lagrange wrote his first paper at the young age of 18, drawing parallels between the Binomial Theorem and the successive derivative of the products of functions. He then wrote several more papers related to calculus. His initial papers had a few drawbacks and clearly demonstrated that Lagrange was working without the guidance of any mathematical supervisor. This made him work even harder.

He is known for his detailed research on the tautochrone, his theories in differential calculus, and for coming up with various differential equations too. Lagrange's theorems are among the basics of calculus now. He also worked with other great mathematicians of his period and came up with several theorems.

47. SHAKUNTALA DEVI

Shakuntala Devi was one of the most amazing women in the 21st century. A genius in her own right, she is known for her calculation and computational abilities. While most of us need calculators or other gizmos to perform simple calculations, she could make some of the most complex calculations mentally within a matter of seconds. She devoted her life towards making basic arithmetic easier and more enjoyable for children.

To understand the brilliance of Shakuntala Devi, we would have to attempt solving the following multiplication problem in seconds without the use of a calculator. What do we get when we multiply 7,686,369,774,870 x 2,465,099,745,779? Most of us wouldn't be able to solve such a complex multiplication problem mentally. She could solve it in seconds at the Imperial College in London! She mentally computed the 23rd root of a 201- digit number in seconds!

No other man or woman was able to do this. In fact, a separate computer program had to be written specifically for this so that simpletons like us could find the answer! She was a child prodigy, and at the age of six, could memorize any sequence of numbers.

She could also correctly tell the day of the week of any date in the last century!

Shakuntala Devi wrote several books like "Puzzles to Puzzle You" and "Book of Numbers" through which she taught people good calculation tricks and made arithmetic easier. Due to cardiac and respiratory problems, she passed away in early 2013, but not before taking the world by storm with her calculation abilities, which took her places!

FAST FACT . . .

It is widely believed that Shakuntala Devi was the fastest human calculator! No computer or calculator can perform the complex calculations faster than she was able to!

48. S. RAMANUJAN

Srinivas Ramanujan is among the most well-known Indian mathematicians of modern times. During a time when India was under the British rule and most Indians, especially those from rural areas, did not receive any formal education or proper exposure to it, Ramanujan stood out and formulated theorems and proofs never seen before. Unfortunately, he died at a very young age. Had he lived longer, he would have revolutionized the world of mathematics!

Due to the lack of exposure that he received, S. Ramanujan was not introduced to the advanced mathematics studies of his time and his knowledge of mathematical methods was also quite limited to the knowledge he gained from the limited resources he had at his disposal.

In spite of all these limitations, he came up with various discoveries and theorems. He came up with a solution to Euler's constant to the 15th decimal place without the

FAST FACT . . .

S Ramanujan was such a genius from early childhood itself, that by the time he was 11, he had already mastered college mathematics books studied by 18-19 year old students.

He moved to London later in life, where he worked with Hardy on several papers. He made important contributions to the analytic theory of numbers, elliptic functions, continued fractions, and infinite series. Due to a prolonged illness, his life was cut short in 1920, when he passed away. However, the world of mathematics continues to honor him for his brilliant work.

knowledge of existent methods for the said purpose. He studied various other fields of geometry and arithmetic in a similar manner. He was rediscovering various theorems by himself without knowing about their existence!

When he found out that a lot of his work had already been formulated or developed before him, he was quite depressed and tried ending his life in London. However, he was saved by his friend and fellow mathematician, G.H. Hardy.

49. PASCAL

In the early 1600s, a French mathematician named Blaise Pascal was born. He was a marvelous mathematician, physicist, and inventor. Apart from his contributions to the field of physics, in which an important unit of pressure has been named after him, he is also known for the invention of the pascaline, a mathematic calculation device that is often considered to be the direct predecessor to the modern day calculator.

Pascal also came up with a series of different inventions. For starters, he invented the most primitive version of the roulette machine, which is popularly seen in casinos today. He was also the first person to wear a wrist watch. He actually attached a string to his pocket watch so that he could wear it around his wrist, making it the first watch of its kind. Apart from this, he authored several papers on different branches of mathematics and physics, including light, sound, pressure, geometry, and algebra.

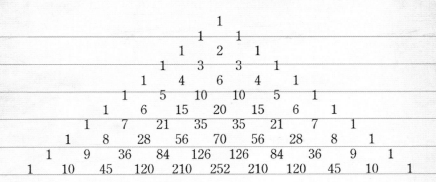

```
                                  1
                              1       1
                          1       2       1
                      1       3       3       1
                  1       4       6       4       1
              1       5      10      10       5       1
          1       6      15      20      15       6       1
      1       7      21      35      35      21       7       1
  1       8      28      56      70      56      28       8       1
1       9      36      84     126     126      84      36       9       1
1      10      45     120     210     252     210     120      45      10      1
```

Pascal's Greatest Invention – The Pascaline

Pascal developed the Pascaline, a bulky device with eight dials connected to each other to add up eight digit long sums while using the base of 10 like we do for carrying out addition today. When the first dial (units place) moved by 10 notches, the second dial (tens place) moved by one notch to show a reading of 10. Similarly when the second (tens) dial moved 10 notches, the third (hundreds) dial moved one notch to show a reading of 100.

This is how it worked and was quite effectively used by his

FAST FACT . . .

In honor of Blaise Pascal, a type of triangle has been named after him. A Pascal triangle is one in which each number in the triangle is the sum of the two numbers above it. It is a very special type of triangle.

father and a lot of other people of the medieval times. This was also the direct predecessor to the modern day calculator.

REASONING

MULTIPLICATION

ADDITION

STATISTICS

DIVISIBILITY

IRRATIONAL NUMBERS

VEDIC MATH

CALCULATING

TRICKS

MASTERING MATH
AND ITS
COMPONENTS

CALCULATOR

LOGIC

STATISTICS

50. VEDIC MATHEMATICS

Vedic mathematics is an ancient Indian system which can be found in some of the oldest scriptures of India. The Vedas which are a treasure trove of knowledge. After being lost in transition for several thousand years, the beauty of the mathematics taught by the Vedas was rediscovered in the early 1900s. Since then, it has been adopted as a wonderful method of teaching students the beauty of mathematics around the world.

The hallmark of Vedic mathematics is the fact that it gives us the opportunity to decide the best way forward by coming up with our own procedures and methods to solve problems. Vedic mathematics has no single "correct" method for solving a problem. Once you develop a basic knowledge and understanding of it, you have the liberty to explore and figure out a comfortable route to solving problems.

In a way, it is extremely simple, flexible, and inventive, giving us an opportunity to learn how to solve complex problems mentally.

According to the teachings of Vedic mathematics, it is believed that mathematics as a whole is based on 16 "sutras" or word formulae. It does not believe that mathematics is divided into different branches like geometry, algebra, and calculus, which are not related to each other. It believes that mathematics is a single subject with everything being interrelated by these 16 formulae. One of these formulae is "Vertically and Cross-wise." People who master this style of mathematics can perform complex calculations in a jiffy! The secrets of Vedic mathematics are being unearthed slowly and steadily and it is believed that the world has a lot more to gain from it.

FAST FACT . . .

In ancient times, Indians had among the most advanced civilizations all over the world. Great mathematicians like Aryabhatta and Brahmagupta, among several others, came up with so many interesting theorems, proofs, and discoveries. Unfortunately, a lot of this knowledge was lost. Slowly and steadily, this knowledge is being regained in modern times through ancient scriptures.

51. MULTIPLICATION TRICKS

Multiplication might often seem difficult, especially when it involves larger numbers. However, there are some handy tricks that you can keep in mind while carrying out multiplication in the case of certain numbers. Read on to make your math life easier! Below are two different tricks that can be used to multiply numbers with five and nine.

The Secret to Multiplication by 9

Multiplication by nine might often be difficult, but not if you know this trick. It is really simple to apply. To multiply any number between one and nine with the number nine, simple cover your face with all your 10 fingers. Now suppose your multiplying 3 by 9, then drop your third finger on your left hand. Now count the number of fingers before this dropped finger (in this case 2) and the number of fingers after it (in this case 7). Now put these numbers together to get the answer, which is 27. Isn't that easy?

Multiplication by 5 Made Easy

This is a trick for the multiplication of five with even numbers. Try multiplying 68 by five. Doesn't seem that easy does it? To use this trick, all you need to know is how to divide the number in half. Divide 68 by two to get the answer and add 0 at the end. On dividing 68 by two, the answer that we get is 34. On adding a 0 at the end of this number, we get 340 as the answer. This is the answer that we get when we multiply 68 by five. Try it out; it always works!

FAST FACT . . .

There is a very interesting fact about dice. The opposite sides of a die always add up to 7.

52. ADDITION TRICKS

Simple arithmetic including addition, subtraction, multiplication, and division, can often take up a lot of our time. In lower classes, this is fine, as we do not need to solve complex problems. But as we keep moving to higher classes, this can prove to be a major challenge, as it is a time consuming affair.

Among the four elementary operations, most of us find addition to be the easiest of the lot. However, even addition can be tough at times, especially if we have to add large numbers. For example, try adding 8766 + 6712. This could take a while. In such cases, it is a good idea to learn certain tricks which would make the entire process of addition a lot easier.

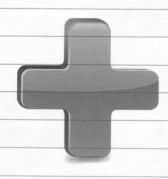

The Method of Partial Sums

The method of partial sums is an easier method for carrying out the addition of higher numbers. Let's take the example of 1237 and 1359. It seems difficult when we see it for the first time. As long as we know the place value system, this method can be quite easy. On adding 1237 and 1359, all we have to do is add up the digits in the units places, tens places, hundreds places, and thousands places separately, and then add them up to get the final answer.

Here is how it works. In the case of the addition of 1237 and 1359, let us see the thousands' place first. The two numbers are 1000 and 1000. Add them up to get 2000. Keep this aside. Now add the numbers in the hundreds' places. These are 200 and 300 which on adding, we get 500. Now, move to the tens' place. On adding, we get 30+50=80. And lastly, move to the ones' place, which gives you 9+7=16. Now add up all these four partial sums. This is the answer we get – 2000 + 500 + 80 + 16 = 2596, which is the answer.

FAST FACT . . .

Armstrong numbers are those in which the sum of the cubes of their individual digits equals to the number itself. There are very few Armstrong numbers. One of them is the number 153.
$1^3 + 5^3 + 3^3 = 153$!

53. EVOLUTION OF CALCULATION

From the time of the abacus in about 300 B.C., there have been several different calculating devices that the world has witnessed before modern day calculators. The evolution of the calculator is very interesting. Human beings have always tried to bring about advancements in the field of mathematical computation and calculation. The calculator that we know today only came into existence around 1892.

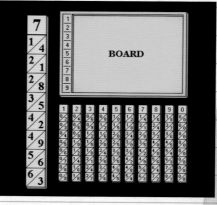

There were a dozen other mathematic devices, starting with the abacus in ancient times up to the Arithmometer in around 1820. By the early 1600s, the concept of the abacus had spread to most parts of Europe and the rest the world. But as mathematics was progressing, the need for a more complex calculating device was felt. John Napier was the first mathematician to attempt it when he came up with "Napier's Bones" for the purpose of multiplication based on the ancient numeral scheme called the Arabian lattice in 1600. Soon, people realized that it was easier to calculate without it!

In 1623, the first mechanical clock, which was an improvement of Napier's device, was developed by German professor Wilhelm Schickard for addition, subtraction, and multiplication. Blaise Pascal's "Pascaline" succeeded this in 1642. Using gear wheels, Leibnitz developed the "Stepped Reckoner," which performed elementary arithmetic operations but failed due to serious mechanical errors.

In 1829, Charles Xavier came up with an "Arithmometer." The "Comptometer," invented in 1884 was the first successful key-driven adding and calculating machine. Finally in 1891, the commercial calculator was developed and manufactured by American inventor William Burroughs, which has undergone tremendous advancements since then.

There is probably a separate and specialized calculator for every different branch of mathematics. They now have cool graphical displays and can perform different complex scientific and mathematical operations.

FAST FACT . . .

The first known "calculator," which is closest to the definition of a modern day calculator, is the Antikethara Device, which was found in the Mediterranean Sea. It was a clockwork astronomical predictor that was almost 2500 years old.

54. COMPUTER VS CALCULATOR

Ever since computers gained popularity in the early 1990s, they reduced the importance of many important scientific and mathematical instruments, as they are capable of carrying out complex calculations by themselves. With the growth of the Internet, the importance of laptops and computers has only increased further, eliminating the need for additional devices.

Texas Instruments came up with the first electronic calculators in 1967. It was considered to be a monumental step in the field of computational devices. It made them less bulky, more portable, and easier to use. The use of calculators increased from then on for the next 30 years.

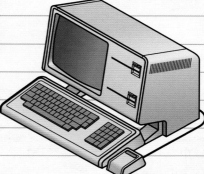

In spite of all this development in the field of calculators, they are no more the instrument of choice for calculation in most cases due to the parallel growth of computers, which offer a variety of different features in addition to those offered by calculators. Apart from this computers are an all-in-one package. As many of us would have observed, computers also provide us with the same facilities and a lot more than calculators do!

Computers let you write, organize schedules, prepare presentations, design, play games, research, listen to music, watch movies, and so much more! People do not feel the need to own a separate calculator, especially when a computer and even a cell

Babbage – Computer

FAST FACT . . .

English mathematician Charles Babbage is considered to be responsible for the birth and development of modern day computers. Around 1812, he carried out several computations of logarithms, which made him realize the inaccuracy that human calculations possess. He set the basis for the development of computers a century later.

phone can calculate for them. The Internet also offers several virtual calculators.

While the use of calculators is on the decline, it is definitely not anytime soon that they will go extinct. They continue to remain significant even today.

55. SCIENCE OF STATISTICS

Another important branch of mathematics is statistics. It deals with the collection, organization, analysis, interpretation, and presentation of data in order to gather structures and detailed information about something. Statistics defines a place for all data and numbers. By placing them and organizing them correctly, it enables us to use this data in a beneficial manner.

Statistics has several different sub-branches that we will learn about in higher grades. The mean, mode, median, etc., are related to statistics. Statistics are used in almost each and every field of work. For example, a lot of us like basketball and the NBA. It has amazing players in different teams. Let's see how statistics helps us decide who the best player is. Basketball players can be judged based on the number of points, rebounds, or assists they make in a game. Though we know how to keep track of points scored per game, how do we find out the details of a player over an entire season? This falls

FAST FACT . . .

Today, statistics has become such a loved subject in mathematics that there are statistics for almost everything. There are statistic for the number of times Lebron James sticks his tongue out while going for a slam dunk!

under the study of statistics. Data over the entire season for every game is collected and compiled. We then find out the points per game (PPG) that a particular player has scored or the season leader for assists, thereby determining the best player. Similarly, statistics is used in several other fields.

56. LOGIC AND REASONING

A very justified question that might strike a lot of us is how logic can be a part of mathematics. Logic is something that we all possess and use to come up with answers or solutions for things. Logic is anything that makes perfect sense. It makes things more sequential and methodical with respect to this branch, which is commonly used in various fields.

Mathematical logic and reasoning is a branch of mathematics that needs to be credited the most for the invention and development of the different technologies that we commonly use today. Working on a computer would have been impossible without mathematical logic and reasoning. Every single thing that we type or view on any computer appears in a particular way due to the fact that they have been programed by making use of mathematical logic and reasoning. Mathematical logic and reasoning includes various sub-branches set theory, model theory, recursion theory, and proof theory.

The reason why several different computational instruments gained importance around the 19th century was because mathematical logic and reasoning became more important. The study of this field became more structured. It was then applied to create programs that led to the development of calculators, computers, mobile phones, and many other commonly used electronic devices today. Mathematical logic and reasoning is also a very

FAST FACT . . .

Even though A is the first letter in the English alphabet, it is quite unfortunate in the number world! In the numbers 0 to 1000, the letter A appears only once, and that too in the number 1000!

important section of different fields of science like physics, where it is used in electronic studies.

57. PUZZLING MATH

Apart from the serious applications of mathematics which are seen in almost every part of life, mathematics is also a common source of recreation and fun. There are a lot of fun games related to mathematics, and puzzles are a nice pastime that keep us engaged and make us think and find the correct solution.

There are several different kinds of mathematical puzzle games. These include puzzles that deal with numbers, arithmetic, and geometry, those that deal with probability, and several other types. A lot of us often spend time playing the game of Sudoku, which is a mathematical puzzle. Another common mathematical puzzle game is Kakuro. These puzzle games originated in South East Asia. Most video games are configured using complex mathematical formulae. They, too, are a type of complex mathematical puzzles.

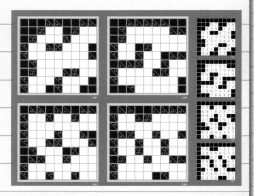

The 24 Puzzle

A popular mathematical puzzle is the "24" puzzle, which is often played in classrooms. The rules of this puzzle are simple. You are given four numbers, which can be any number between one and nine.

You are allowed to carry out any elementary operation on them (addition, subtraction, multiplication, or division) to obtain the final answer - 24. Let us take an example of this. Assume that the four numbers given to you are 7, 8, 8, and 4. What operations do you carry out on these numbers to get 24 as the answer? The answer is $(8/8+7) \times 3 = 24$.

FAST FACT . . .

40, written as forty, is the only number which has its letters in an alphabetical order! No other number has its successive letters in a perfect alphabetical order like the number 40.

58. PARTING THE WHOLE

Fractions are an important part of mathematics. They deal with numbers that are not considered to be "whole numbers." Fractions have been in use since ancient times, and are also used by us during our daily conversations. Be it arithmetic, geometry, or calculus, fractions are an essential part of every branch of mathematics.

Fractions are made up of two types of numbers. They are the numerator, which is the number on top, and the denominator, which is the number at the bottom. These two numbers are separated by a "/" symbol or a line between them. For example, "5/8" is a fraction in which the number 5 is the numerator and the number 8 is the denominator. A fraction always indicates a part of the whole, where the numerator indicates the part and the denominator represents the whole. In this case, the numerator is 5, which means we are talking about 5 parts of the whole number.

The denominator is 8, which means the whole number in this case is 8. So, we are talking about 5 parts of 8. Other fractions are also written in a similar manner.

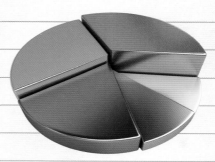

FAST FACT . . .

The number one and every positive integer that follows it belong to a set called whole numbers. All whole numbers have predecessors that are also whole numbers. However, zero stands out in this crowd as it is the only number without a whole number as a predecessor.

Some different kinds of fractions are proper fractions, improper fractions, mixed fractions, and several others. Fractions are a common part of our normal conversations as well. For example, when you tell someone that you are running late by half an hour, you are using the fraction "half."

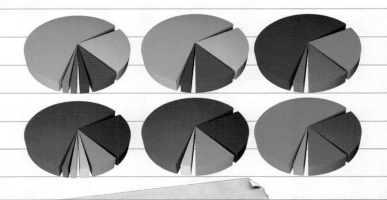

59. IRRATIONAL MATH

The concept of rational and irrational numbers has been an integral part of mathematics ever since mathematicians started making complex calculations. There were always some numbers and calculations which seemed to be a lot tougher to carry out, while most others were relatively easier to deal with. Thus, the concept of rational and irrational numbers was born.

Irrational numbers are those which cannot be expressed as whole numbers or fractions. They can be expressed in decimal form but their final answer is inconclusive, which means that it is never ending. Rational numbers, on the other hand, can be expressed as a whole number or in a fractional form.

The square root of 2 is an irrational number. Similarly, Euler's constant, which is roughly 2.71, is also irrational. There are other common irrational numbers, like the Golden Ratio, which is roughly 1.61.

There is an interesting story behind the discovery of the concept of irrational numbers. A Pythagorean student called Hippasus discovered the concept of irrational numbers while trying to find out the square root of 2. Instead of finding the square root of 2, he realized that there were

some numbers which were not real and did not have a definite value, such that they could not be represented as fractions either. This was the birth of the concept of real numbers. However, Pythagoras believed that every number must have a real value and did not agree with Hippasus, who was apparently thrown overboard and drowned.

60. DIVISIBILITY TESTS

Mathematics is full of numbers that can be divided by other numbers to give whole number values. The basic numbers, using which other numbers can be divided, are 1 to 9. Certain divisibility tests make it easier to decide if a particular number can be divided by any of these numbers. They are very easy to learn and will make math life so much easier!

Divisibility test for 1

Every whole number is divisible by 1. On dividing a number by 1, the answer we get is the number itself. For example, 4,567,921 divided by 1 is 4,567,921 itself!

Divisibility test for 2

To find out if a particular number is divisible by 2, all we need to know is whether that particular number is odd or even. All even numbers are divisible by 2 while all odd numbers are not. For example, 64 is divisible by 2 as it is an

even number, while 63 is not, as it is an odd number.

Divisibility test for 3

To check if a particular number is divisible by 3, all we need to do is add up the digits of the number.

FAST FACT . . .

Follow the given steps to look like a genius. Ask your friends to think of any number in their minds. Ask them to subtract 1 from the given number. The answer must be multiplied by 3. Then, ask them to add 12 to the result. The answer must be divided by 3, and 5 must be added to the resultant answer. Now from this resultant answer, subtract the original number thought of. The answer will always be 8!

If the number obtained by adding the digits of the number is divisible by 3, then the original number is also divisible by 3. For example, let us check if 531 is divisible by 3. The sum of the digits of 531 are 9, which is divisible by 3 as 3 x 3 is equal to 9. Hence, 531 is also divisible by 3. Try to test if 566 is divisible by 3 using the same test.

FAST FACT . . .

There are only two prime numbers that end with the number 2 and 5, and these are 2 and 5 themselves! Try thinking of another prime number of this sort, you definitely won't find one!

61. DIVISIBILITY TESTS

We've already learnt the divisibility test tricks for 1, 2, and 3. Let us now learn the divisibility tests for 4, 5, and 9. Unfortunately, the divisibility test for 7 is quite complicated and too difficult to learn.

Divisibility test for 4

For a number to be divisible by 4, the number formed by its last 2 digits should be divisible by 4. For example, 432 is divisible by 4 as the number formed by its last 2 digits is divisible by 4 as 4 x 8 = 32.

Divisibility test for 5

5 has one of the easiest divisibility tests. If the last digit of a particular number is either 5 or 0, then it is divisible by 5. If someone asks you if 12344431798689625 is divisible by 5, you don't need to look at the entire number. Just look at the last digit which is 5.
The number is divisible by 5. Simple, isn't it?

9

Divisibility test for 9

To find out if a particular number is divisible by 9, we need to see if the sum of its digits is divisible by 9. For example, let us take the number 657. The sum of the digits of this number is 18, which is divisible by 9, as 9x2=18. Hence, 657 is divisible by 9.

FAST FACT . . .

Any number that is divisible by three and four and greater than 12 will always be divisible by the number 12 as well. You can give this a try with any number. Try it on 36, 108, and 72 to begin with!

12

FAST FACT . . .

In order for a number to be divisible by 11, the difference between the sum of the odd numbered digits and the even numbered digits should be divisible by 11 or should be 0. Try it out for any multiple of 11!

11

SEVEN

BODMAS

CONE

SPHERE

POLYGON

TRIANGLES

CIRCLES

SQUARES

THE BEAUTY OF SHAPES AND NUMBERS

RECTANGLES

THIRTEEN

62. WONDROUS ONE

For more reasons than one, the number 1 can be called the most unique number of all. It is probably for that very reason that it is given more importance than most numbers, even when we rank people, events, teams, or anything else.

used by the Indians. With the passing of time, it switched from a horizontal line to a curved line and finally became a vertical line. Ancient Chinese civilizations referred to the number one by making use of a horizontal line.

For thousands of years, "one" was the only number that man used for the purpose of counting. The original symbol for the number one was a horizontal line, which was

FAST FACT . . .

The number one is also called a multiplicative identity, as any number multiplied by one gives the value of the number itself as the answer. For example, 872 x 1 = 872.

18

FAST FACT . . .

18 is the only positive number that is equal to the value of twice the sum of its digits. The two digits in 18 are 1 and 8, which add up to 9. On doubling 9, we get 18.

One is literally one in a million! On multiplying it with any number, it does not change the number, which would not be the case if we try and multiply any number with other numbers. Similarly, it does not change the value of a number when it divides the number which, again, is not the case with any other number. The square, square root, cube, and cube root of one is one itself!

One is the first positive odd number. Even though it is not divisible by any number apart from itself, it is not considered a prime number. It is actually considered to be a unique number, which is neither prime nor composite.

63. THE MAGIC OF THREE

There is something very special about each and every number, but there are some numbers that are more special than others. The number three happens to be one of them. It is of great significance in many different cultures and in philosophy as well. There are some extremely interesting facts about the number three that make it so special. What is more astounding to note is that three seems to be significant in every walk of life.

height. Objects that appear flat to us are actually three–dimensional. There are three primary colors – red, yellow, and blue. All other colors have been derived from these three colors. Earth is the third planet from the Sun.

Three is the first odd prime number which cannot be divided by any other number apart from itself. In many

Three is everywhere. There are three dimensions for every object-length, width, and

FAST FACT . . .

An interesting fact about 81 is that it is one of the only numbers equal to the sum of the squares of its digits. The sum of its digits is 9. The square of 9 is 81!

FAST FACT . . .

This is an interesting trick to try on your friends. For any number below 10, the answer for this trick is always 3. Tell your friends to choose a number below 10. Then, ask them to double it and add 6 to the result. The answer so obtained must be halved (divided by 2). Tell them to subtract the original number they thought of from the answer they got. The final answer will always be 3! Give it a try!

cultures, it is believed that there are three worlds – heaven, earth, and the underworld. It is believed that the Gods live in heaven, humans live on Earth, and demons live in the underworld.

An entire branch of mathematics is named after three – Trigonometry. "Tri," of course, refers to three. The study of triangles (three sides) of different types is significant, and several mathematicians have dedicated their entire lives to it.

64. SUPER SEVEN

The number seven plays a significant role in various fields like religion and spirituality. It is also an important part of the number system, physics, and chemistry. Different aspects of time studies are also related to the number seven.

to mind is that there are seven colors in a rainbow — violet, indigo, blue, green, yellow, orange, and red.

When we think about the number seven, the first thing that probably comes to our mind is that there are seven days in a week. Another common thought that comes

FAST FACT . . .

Have you ever wondered what comes after a million, billion, and trillion? The entire series of numbers is never ending. Quadrillion, quintillion, sextillion, septillion, octillion, nonillion, decillion, and undecillion are the next few numbers, which appear with a string of zeros attached to them!

The Earth is divided into seven continents. There are seven musical syllables – do, re, me, fa, so, la, and ti. We often talk about the seven wonders of the world. The Indian culture states that there are seven "chakras" or points in the body. The moon is believed to have seven phases. Seventh heaven is believed, by some religions, to be the purest place.

The heart has seven compartments and the brain has seven natural divisions. There are numerous other places where seven is highly important. "Secret Seven" is a series of books written by renowned author, Enid Blyton.

FAST FACT . . .

Around 2,500 years ago, writers in Ancient Greece started making lists of the seven must-see "sights" in the world, which are now called the "Seven Wonders of the Ancient World." The winners were announced on 07/07/2007!

65. UNLUCKY 13

13 is supposedly an unlucky number. Having been unnecessarily given a bad name due to a series of unfortunate circumstances in its case, most people like to keep away from it. However, there is enough reason to believe that 13 is not so bad. There are several important things related to 13. Let's get to know what made 13 so unlucky!

13

FAST FACT . . .
Some hotels and hospitals often skip the number 13 on their rooms and floors. The elevators take you from the 12th floor to the 14th floor. Even airports often conveniently skip 13 while numbering terminals!

There is a huge conspiracy theory surrounding the number 13. It is often said to be evil and unlucky. Whether this is true or not is probably going to be debated upon for eternity, but we can hope for the sake of the number 13 that this is probably not the case.

Not everybody considers poor 13 to be unlucky. There are several countries in Africa and Asia where 13 is considered to

That's how it came to be known as unlucky 13.

be auspicious and lucky too. Many parts of the United States of America consider it to be very special. In fact, the first US national flag had 13 stripes to represent the 13 different colonies. Even today, it has 13 stars.

It is believed that Friday the 13th began to be considered unlucky because it was on Friday, the 13th in 1307 that several knights in France were arrested and unjustly killed. Poor 13 therefore came to be associated with bad luck and became an unlucky date through no fault of its own!

FAST FACT . . .

Friday, the 13th

Friday, the 13th is a popular date in media and culture. It is considered to be a day of horrors and quite inauspicious. It is the title of a famous horror movie that released in 2009. Geoffrey Chaucer's great book "Canterbury Tales" written in the 14th century can also be credited for Friday, the 13th receiving such a bad name!

66. TOP 10

While listing different numbers which have quite a lot of significance in our daily lives, we must mention the number 10. It forms the base for most mathematical calculations and computations today. The usage of 10 has made mathematics so much easier than it was in earlier times. A flexible and versatile number, it is among the easiest to use for elementary operations like addition, subtraction, multiplication, and division. It is commonly used in our daily lives too.

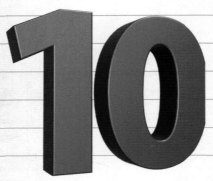

to count up to the number 10. Even when it comes to any listing or order of ranking, we always start counting toward the top from the number 10. All countdowns begin with 10. In several different competitions and tests, scores are generally given out of 10. Getting 10 on 10 is an important goal that a lot of us set for ourselves!

It would be safe to say that irrespective of how educated a person is, almost every single person in the world learns how

In the field of mathematics, 10 is considered extremely flexible and easy to use.

FAST FACT . . .

Here's another cool trick you can try on your friends. Tell them to think of any three digit number in which all the three digits are the same (E.g. 333, 444). Now tell them to add up the three digits of the number. Once they have done this, tell them divide the three digit number by the number obtained by adding its digits up. The answer they will get every single time is 37! Amazing, isn't it?

When we multiply a number by 10, all we need to do is add a zero at the end of it to get the answer. When we divide a number by 10, all we have to do is remove a zero or place a decimal point before the last number. A lot of calculations are done using 10 as a base. Logarithms to the base of 10 are also quite commonly used.

67. BODMAS

While performing mathematical calculations, we are often required to carry out addition, multiplication, division, and subtraction simultaneously. The challenge that we face in such cases is to decide where to start off. Depending upon where we start which elementary operation we start with, the answer differs. Hence, it is very important to know the order in which we must carry out such calculations.

The rule of BODMAS can be best understood by looking at the following example. Consider that you have to solve the following problem:
13 x 8/2 + 5 - 4

It is very important to understand the order laid down in mathematics for carrying out different mathematical operations. This order can easily be remembered by memorizing the word "BODMAS," which is an abbreviation for Bracket

FAST FACT . . .
111111111 x 111111111 = 12345678987654321.
Math is a very beautiful subject, weaving numbers into beautiful patterns, as the one shown above, where numbers progressively increase from 1 to 9 and then decrease from 9 to 1.

Order Division Multiplication Addition and Subtraction.

BODMAS is an abbreviation that tells the order in which we must carry out elementary operations. These operations have to be carried out in the order in which their names appear in this abbreviation. As division appears before multiplication, division must be carried out before multiplication. Similarly, addition must be carried out before subtraction. On using the rules of BODMAS, the answer that we receive for the given problem is 53. BODMAS is an important concept in mathematics that we must remember.

FAST FACT . . .

Four seconds is the average time that an internet user generally waits for a page to load. After that, they generally refresh and try to reload the page.

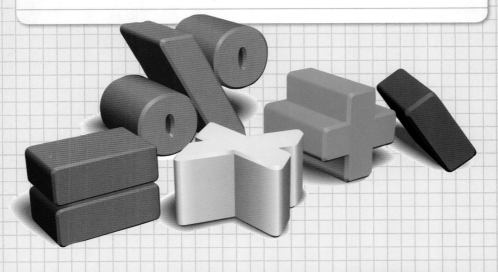

68. GEOMETRIC SHAPES

It is believed that each shape in geometry has its own significance. Just like numbers, different geometric shapes also indicate different things. They instill different feelings in us in a subconscious manner. Additionally, different shapes are also significant in cultures and religions around the world, such as the triangle.

In geometry, shapes are basically two dimensional areas with a recognizable boundary. There are two very distinct features that make up a shape,

FAST FACT . . .

A famous man once rightfully said, "Math is no different from life. It is full of problems. But there is a solution to every single problem!"

FAST FACT . . .

The word geometry is derived from two Greek words – "geo," which means Earth and "metria," meaning measure. Hence, geometry actually means to measure the Earth. Mathematicians have sure done way more than that over thousands of years!

namely the color that we fill them up with, which is different from that of their surroundings and the lines that form their edges. Shapes can be like regular polygons or free in form.

69. CONES

Cones are another important three-dimensional shape in geometry. Possessing a variety of unique properties, cones are used for making several different objects that are used for important applications. Cones, as a shape, are also used to construct buildings and various other structures. They possesses several advantages over other shapes, which can be utilized for our benefit!

The cone is a three-dimensional shape which all of us may have seen and loved – the ice cream cone! Aren't cones delicious? They are important too!

A cone is actually a three-dimensional shape which tapers smoothly from the base and ends in a point at the top. The bottom of a cone is always in the shape of a circle. Finding the volume and area of a cone is important in mathematics. It helps to obtain the solution for many different problems.

FAST FACT . . .
One of the most common devices used to obtain the colors of a rainbow from regular white light is a prism. A triangular prism has a square base with two sides being rectangles and the other two sides being equilateral triangles.

70. CIRCLE

The circle is one of the most easily identifiable geometric shapes. Commonly used in many day-to-day applications, it conveys a certain set of emotions which are characteristic to it. It was also among the first shapes created by humans in ancient times. The major feelings conveyed by circles are those of fullness and security. Circular objects are also easier to transport.

The great thing about circles is that they neither have a beginning nor an end. The most commonly seen circular objects are wheels, balls, and fruits of several different kinds. Circles are known for their free movement because circular objects have the ability to roll. Thus, they are seen as more easily accessible too. Their easy movement conveys emotions like grace, comfort, energy, and power. Their roundness is a complete figure that conveys emotions like being infinite, or a symbol for peace and harmony.

The rounded shape of circles gives people a sense of protection, as they believe that they are engulfed in a circle that protects them from all over. They are also looked upon as restrictive, as they can confine something. In some cultures, circles are believed to convey integrity and perfection too.

The common saying, "life has come to a full circle" means that life has come back to where it began.

Circles are used commonly in design as compared to rectangles and squares. They are used for providing emphasis to designs, for attracting attention, and setting things apart.

FAST FACT . . .

The toughest signature that a person can have is believed to be a circle. It is considered impossible to repeat the same circle a second time if drawn freehand. Trying to draw one without a compass is anyways quite a difficult proposition! You should probably think about making this your signature! It will remain secure for life. However, you might never be able to use it again!

71. RECTANGLES AND SQUARES

Rectangles and squares are the most commonly seen shapes in daily life. Just look around you to realize how rectangles and squares surround you. Right from the shape of your beds to the shape of the refrigerators and probably even the air conditioners. Most vehicles are also rectangular shaped. Most boxes that we use are generally square or rectangular in shape. Both these shapes convey a set of emotions and moods.

Squares and rectangles are believed to convey a sense of stability as they are present in most environments known to us. They are believed to represent honesty due to our familiarity with them. They represent

FAST FACT . . .

Among all the different four-sided figures, squares have the largest area for a given length of sides. In other words, no matter which four-sided figure we decide to draw, be it a rectangle or a tetrahedron, the area of a square will be maximum if the sum of the lengths of their sides is equal.

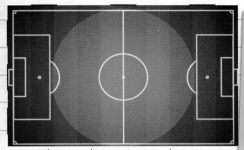

Cristiano Ronaldo is one of the greatest soccer players on the planet today. He has the unique distinction of scoring in every single minute of a soccer match except for the 47th minute! He sure does keep track of time!

order, mathematics, and rationality too. Rectangles are definitely the most commonly seen shape. Squares are seen less commonly and are simply modified forms of rectangles in which all sides are equal. Due to their equal sides, squares are believed to represent a sense of perfection.

The first representation of any house or place that we make is rectangular as well. Most conventional playgrounds, courts, etc., are also rectangular in shape. It is the shape that we are inherently habituated to making use of for a variety of things. Today, rectangles and squares are used by designers to such a large extent that they are now looking for alternative shapes that can be used. This is a move to be unconventional because human beings are so used to seeing rectangles and squares.

72. TRIANGLE RULES

Triangles are the most important field in mathematics, with an entire branch in mathematics (trigonometry) being devoted to them. Great mathematicians have spent their entire lives studying the unique properties of the triangle.

To make a shape, a minimum of three points are required to be joined. A single point represents a dot and joining two points will give us a line. Trigonometry is the study of triangles. In fact, it is more specifically the study of right-angled triangles.

The properties of triangles are so vast and unique, they can be used to find out heights, distances, and positions of various objects in space. The hypotenuse of a right-angled triangle is considered the shortest distance between two points.

FAST FACT . . .

The triangle is the most preferred shape used for the construction of buildings, etc. It is believed to impart structural strength and sturdiness that no other shape can provide.

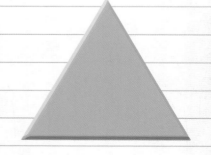

73. ON CLOUD NINE

Just like some of the other single digit numbers, there are many events and things related to the number 9. Mathematically, the number 9 is very interesting, with it being an important field of study for many mathematicians.

If you multiply any number from 1 to 10 by 9 and add the digits, the sum will be 9! Additionally, the sum of the digits of any number that is added to the number 9 is always equal to the sum of the digits of the answer. For example, 11+9 = 20 (1+1=2 and 2+0=2).

9 is also related to emotions like extreme happiness. Being on "cloud nine" means that you are ecstatic! Did you know that on an average, every school functions for nine months in a year? There are also several other interesting facts related to the number 9. A standard work day is from 9 am to 5 pm. Most offices begin their day at 9 am!

FAST FACT . . .

Harmony in music occurs when two pitches vibrate at frequencies in small integer ratios. The notes of middle G and high C sound good together because the latter has twice the frequency of the former. G and C are in a ratio of 3:2. Therefore, notes are created by calculating their frequency!

74. HEXAGONS

Hexagons form an important part of geometric studies, as they are closely associated with triangles. It is also a shape that occurs naturally as a part of various plant and animal parts. It is the most preferred shape with more than four sides.

Hexagons derive their name from the Greek word "hexa" which means six, as they are six-sided. Six equilateral triangles,

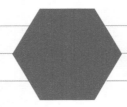

when brought together, form a regular hexagon.

Many plant cells have a hexagonal structure. Honeycombs are hexagonal. The Giant's Causeway in Northern Ireland has 40,000 interlocked basalt columns which are hexagonal. Many geometric patterns used for designs have hexagons. This shape is also commonly seen in footballs.

FAST FACT . . .

All odd numbers are obtained as the sum of an odd number and an even number. No odd number can be obtained by adding two even numbers or two odd numbers. Why don't you give this a try? Note that zero is neither an even number nor an odd number.

75. THE SPHERE OF LIFE!

The most common regular three-dimensional object is probably a sphere. Spheres are seen everywhere. This three-dimensional shape is also probably the source of our existence. Along with cones and cylinders, spheres are commonly seen in various daily applications. Apart from this, the universe is also filled with spherical objects.

A sphere is a perfectly round three-dimensional shape with absolutely no edges. Every point on the surface of a sphere is at the same distance from the center.

The sphere is considered to be an important shape as it is the shape of Earth, which houses the plant kingdom, animal kingdom, mineral kingdom, human beings, and every possible object in the world. Other celestial bodies such as planets, Sun, and moon are also spherical in shape.

Almost every single sport is played with a ball, be it basketball, soccer, or even baseball. Football is one of the few sports that isn't played with a spherical ball.

Imagine what we would have done without spheres! It is the most mobile shape. It can be transported with utmost ease.

LIGHT YEARS

LATITUDE

EQUATOR

BARCODE

RICHTER SCALE

ZIP CODE

COMPUTER LANGUAGE

NUMBERS

COUNTDOWN

EQUATOR

NUMBERS IN OUR DAILY LIVES

SCORE

BINGO

LONGITUDE

76. FANTASTIC FOUR

The magic of four is unique and quite special. It has great significance in different fields of mathematics, such as geometry. It also has some special characteristic features in mathematics that no other number possesses. Four-sided geometric figures are also of immense importance.

Four-sided figures such as the tetrahedron, square, and rectangle are an integral part of geometry. The properties of these four-sided figures are used to solve many different problems.

The number "four" is also referred to as "tetra" and "quad." Four is the only number that has the same number of letters as the actual number itself. No other number shares this unique feature!

Four is also of immense importance in geometry.

FAST FACT . . .
A "googloplex" is the number 1 followed by "googol" zeros. "Googol" is a number that is so big that there is not enough space in the entire universe to fit it!

77. CALL ME!

A "telephone number" or just "phone number" is a unique sequence of numbers that is used to connect one telephone line to another on a phone network. In the beginning, people had only one number. Nowadays, every other person has a cell phone, a landline and an office phone and numbers often run into 10 digits.

Area and National Codes

With the advent of worldwide calling, we need to distinguish between numbers in different areas and countries. This has led to national and area codes being defined. A national code has two digits and is generally written as "+XX." Area codes don't have any specific format. They range from one digit to five.

FAST FACT . . .

"Hello, is this God?"
When the 2003 movie "Bruce Almighty" was released, the number shown on screen for God was dialed by many filmgoers as a prank.

Your call charges are also decided by the area and national code you dial before the number. If you don't specify an area and national code, by default the phone assumes it to be your area.

78. T MINUS 10

The phrase "T Minus" is most famously associated with rocket launches or races. Here, "T" generally stands for "Time" or "Test."

The idea behind this is to count backwards to a certain event. When the count reaches zero, the event starts – be it a race, a launch, the New Year, or any other such event. Since we are counting down to zero, this practice is commonly known as a countdown.

Countdowns have existed for over 2000 years now. The biggest example of a countdown is the naming of years in the Gregorian calendar. The oldest known instrument for measuring a countdown is an hourglass. The time is signified as "until the turn of the glass," i.e., until the sand runs out.

Today, we use countdown timers of various types for different purposes. An oven or a microwave is used to set the cooking time. The alarm you set is a countdown to the time you have to wake up.

FAST FACT . . .
When we moved from the 20th century to the 21st at the end of 1999, computers faced what was known as the Y2K problem.

79. KEEPING SCORE

We've all heard the phrase, "friends don't keep score." Keeping a score or a tally is just another way of counting, generally by assigning a value to an event.

Some games, like chess or battleship, have a single objective – capture the king, kill all of the opponent's pieces, capture the flag, etc. The first person to fulfill this objective wins. But what about games that have a time based ending, like football, soccer, basketball? How do you determine the winner in a game like that? Basically you keep score.

Games such as racing have a different form of scoring. You're supposed to cover a given distance in the least amount of time. Whoever finishes earliest, that is, with the lowest score wins. Many card games have a similar system. At the end of each round, the value of cards remaining in your hand are tallied and added to your previous score.

FAST FACT . . .
In China, the number 14 is so inauspicious that any proposal that receives 14 votes in favor would automatically fail, regardless of how many were against it!

FAST FACT . . .
666 is considered to be the devil's number and called "the mark of the beast."

80. LONGITUDE AND LATITUDE

To avoid confusion, Earth has been divided by a set of parallel lines that run horizontally and vertically around it. Any place on Earth can be located by specifying which horizontal and vertical line it lies on.

The Longitude is a vertical line running from the North Pole to the South Pole. The Latitude is a horizontal line circling the globe parallel to the equator.
The idea of Latitude and Longitude was first proposed by Eratosthenes in the third century B.C. It was further developed by Hipparchus and Ptolemy, who used it to specify

FAST FACT . . .

Did you know that it is possible to have one foot in Sunday and another in Monday? There is an imaginary line called the International Date Line. The date changes as you cross the line. If you cross from East to West, you gain a day and vice versa.

the location of cities. Today the system is so well-developed that it is possible to differentiate between two different windows in the same house! The latitude can be more or less determined by the position of the Sun at noon along with the date since the Sun appears to move with the season. Longitude, on the other hand, is more difficult to determine and define.

Another important function that the longitude serves is telling time. As you can imagine, it is not the same time of the day in Japan and Germany. Based on longitude, the world is divided into 23 different time zones. The time in Greenwich is said to be GMT (Greenwich Mean Time) and time is added as you move east and subtracted as you move west.

FAST FACT . . .

A paper can never be folded more than nine times no matter how hard you try! Give it a try.

81. CAR NAME

Just like we have names to identify us, cars have Vehicle Identification Numbers. This number is like a permanent name given to a car.

Car names are legally required for the VIN and are an integral part of the vehicle, i.e., it can't just be removed or replaced like your license plate. The VIN is also present on all your vehicle registration papers.

The VIN number is a 17 digit number standardized across the world by car manufacturers. VINs were first used in

FAST FACT . . .
Every phone has a unique IMEI (International Mobile Station Equipment Identity) number. If your phone is lost or stolen, communicate the number to your service provider and they'll ensure that no service provider gives access to a SIM (Subscriber Identity Module) card in that handset.

FAST FACT . . .
There is a very famous riddle which goes, "What is half a circle, full circle, half circle, A. Half circle, full circle, right angle, A?" The answer, of course, is Coca Cola!

1954. However, there was no accepted standard from 1954 to 1981. The International Standard Organisation (ISO) set a standard format for the 17 digits in 1979 through ISO 3779:2009. This format uses a combination of letters and numbers.

82. BINGO!

Have you heard of people who believe that certain numbers are suited to them? They'll buy lottery cards and bingo tickets with those numbers. Some choose their phone numbers, license plates and sometimes even their home address based on this! These people are ardent followers of a practice called numerology.

Initially many prominent mathematicians like Dirac and Descartes were attracted to numerology to explain certain trends and mathematical observations. However, today numerology is considered a "pseudoscience" and its practitioners treated as charlatans by the scientific community.

FAST FACT . . .

Triskaidekaphobia refers to the fear of the number "thirteen." Due to this, many establishments do not have a 13th floor or room number 13. Besides, there also are phobias like tetraphobia, which is fear of the number "4."

Numerologists also believe that each person has a "cardinal number" that best describes them, based on their time and place of birth.

83. EQUATOR

The Equator is an imaginary line drawn at the center of the Earth by humans. The line is not physically drawn. Therefore you will never be able to actually see it!

FAST FACT . . .
Each day is 86,400 seconds long! Doesn't this make each day seem so much longer?

The equator is the 0 degree latitude line. This imaginary line is the midpoint between the North Pole and the South Pole. Because the equator is half way between the North and South poles, we use it to divide the Earth into two equal halves – the Northern and Southern Hemispheres.

FAST FACT . . .
Believe it or not, ABCDEF is an actual number. In the hexadecimal system (having 16 digits instead of the usual 10), in addition to 0-9, we have an additional 6 digits A-F. This system is generally used in computers.

Therefore, the equator is used as a point to help us define where things are on Earth. The equator is what enables scientists and researchers to judge our location on the planet. This is how they can say that a specific place is a certain distance "above" or "below" the equator!

84. CAN COMPUTERS TALK?

The use of computers has revolutionized education. Many child-friendly computer programing languages have also evolved. Computer programing languages are all different series of numbers.

A computer programming language is a language created by us, to control the computer by performing various functions. These languages enable the user to communicate with the computer and tell it what to do. Although there are over 2,000 computer languages, relatively few are widely used.

High-level languages shield a programer from worrying

about such considerations and provide a notification that is more easily written and read by programers. Therefore, the commands that we write are shown as numbers to the computer, which then carries out the appropriate function.

85. LIGHT-YEARS

The distance in space is way more than that on Earth. Therefore it is not measured in miles or meters, but in light-years!

The nearest star is about 24 trillion miles away or about 24,000,000,000,000 miles away. If someone wanted to solve a math problem with that number it would be very difficult.

To make this number smaller and easier to work with, we use something called "light-years." Just like using miles instead of feet makes the number above smaller, using light-years instead of miles makes numbers smaller.

FAST FACT . . .

In many races or games where people bet, odds are offered against or for a particular competitor. Odds of 5:1 mean that the horse is 5 times as likely to lose as he is to win. So, a dollar bet on the horse would pay out five if he won.

FAST FACT . . .

It takes three minutes for light to travel between Mars and Earth when the two planets are closest to each other!

One light-year equals to about 6 trillion miles (6,000,000,000,000).

86. WAIT A SECOND!

Everyone knows that a year is the time taken for the Earth to circle the Sun once, and a day is the time taken for the Earth to circle itself once. What about a minute or a second?

FAST FACT . . .
It is possible to cut a pie into eight pieces with only three cuts. Give this a try!

Time was measured based on a sexagesimal system since the time of the ancient Egyptians. That is why a minute was 60 seconds, an hour was 60 minutes, and a day was 24 hours.

Based on this, early astronomers had defined a second as 1/86400th of a day. However, not everyday is exactly the same.

Today, a second is defined as the duration of 9,192,631,770 periods of the radiation corresponding to the transition between the two hyperfine levels of the ground state of the caesium-133 atom. Phew!

FAST FACT . . .
We blink our eyes every 300 to 400 milliseconds. It is a reflex action meaning it happens automatically without us having to make an effort to do it.

87. EXTRAPOLATION

Extrapolation is the process of predicting by projecting past experience or known data and comparing its percentage or ratio.

Extrapolation of data is used in places where a part of the data is given and the rest must be predicted. For example, when driving, a driver guesses the condition of the road ahead based on that of the road he's already crossed. It is based on the idea that all phenomena or events display a certain characteristic behavior or trend.

FAST FACT . . .

The mathematical compass is not only used for making circles or cutting angles. It is possible to use the compass to draw straight and slanting lines just like a ruler! We only use a ruler for the sake of convenience!

FAST FACT . . .

The concept of a triple double is something that comes from basketball. When a player makes more than 10 rebounds, 10 assists, and 10 points in a single game, he secures a triple double.

There are many methods of extrapolation that are used, depending on how much data is available and how accurately we wish to calculate the next data.

88. RICHTER SCALE

In 1935, the Richter magnitude scale was developed by Charles F. Richter at the California Institute of Technology as a method to compare the sizes of earthquakes. Initially, it was designed to be used with only one instrument that Richter used in his lab. However, the method was so successful that it is used widely even today.

The Richter scale uses the amplitude of oscillations as a measure of how severe an earthquake is. That's just another way of saying that it measures how much objects are shaken by a given earthquake. Richter magnitude is a number with one digit after the decimal place. The scale is logarithmic — this means that 3 on the scale is 10 times as severe as 2 but only 1/10th of 4 and so on.

FAST FACT . . .

The largest earthquake that was ever recorded on a Richter scale measures to 9.5. Known as the Valdivia earthquake or the Great Chilean Earthquake, it occurred in 1960.

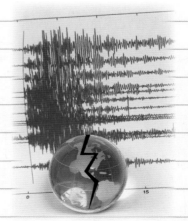

89. THE PIGEONHOLE PRINCIPLE

If there are 7 pigeonholes and 8 pigeons given to you, can you place one pigeon in each hole? After you've put the first 7 pigeons in a hole, you have one pigeon left. This mathematical principle is called the pigeonhole principle.

It is believed that the idea was first proposed by Peter Gustav Lejeune Dirichlet in 1834 under the name "Schubfachprinzip" ("drawer principle" or "shelf principle"). It is one of the basic principles of counting and has various trivial and non-trivial applications.

FAST FACT . . .
The age of the Earth is estimated to be 4,540,000,000 years! The age of the Sun is 5 billion years!

The trivial applications include various puzzles. For example, you have 3 pairs of socks in your wardrobe. In the dark, how many must you pick up to ensure that you have at least one pair? Or, if there are 450 people at a party, what are the chances that two of them share a birthday?

90. KELVIN

The SI (International System) unit of temperature is named Kelvin after British engineer and physicist William Thomson (1824-1907), the first Baron of Kelvin.

Unlike Fahrenheit or Celsius, Kelvin is not preceded by the term "degree." This is because Kelvin is an absolute scale and not relative to anything.

The previous units of temperature, the Fahrenheit and Celsius, were both based on the freezing and boiling points of water. This is not a constant temperature – water boils at different temperatures in different places. Therefore, Lord Kelvin decided to use a more fixed point as zero. He picked the coldest temperature possible as the starting point for the scale. This temperature is known as "absolute zero" and is 273.16 degrees below the freezing point of water. Yes, 0 K (Kelvin) is equal to -523.688° F.

FAST FACT . . .

The Sun has an effective surface temperature of approximately 5800 K, which makes it look yellow. In a few billion years, the Sun will expand and cool down, first turning orange and then red.

91. COUNTING

The fundamental principle of counting is a technique that accounts for all probable ways to carry out one activity. The rule of product is essential in calculating probabilities.

This fundamental principle determines the total number of ways for events to occur, assuming that no two events can happen at the same time. For example, say you are traveling from USA to Russia, and stopping by England on the way. If there are two ways from USA to England and 3 from England to Russia, how many different paths can you take? Let's say USA to England has paths A and B and England to Russia has C, D, and E. You can use AC, AD, AE, BC, BD, and BE. Clearly, you can reach Russia using six different paths.

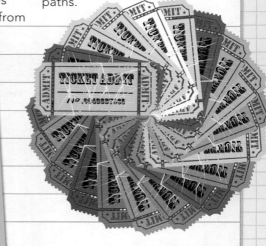

FAST FACT . . .

In Canada, a winner of sweepstakes has to correctly answer a math question before he/she can claim the prize money. It is generally a simple three-four line problem involving addition, subtraction, multiplication, and division.

FAST FACT . . .

People use Math to Win a Lottery!

Joan Gither of Texas has won the lottery there 4 times! The chances of this are more than one in a septabillion and it is actually no coincidence! Joan is a PhD in Math and has apparently figured out a method or formula to do this! Of course, she has not disclosed it to anyone!

92. GOOGLE IT!

Google is unarguably the most famous company on earth at this point in time. It is also quite possibly the most famous company ever, having become the byword for searching any information.

The funny thing is, it never would've come into existence if someone hadn't misspelled a word on Google's first ever paycheck. The name Google is derived from the word "googol" which is a number that is 10^{100} i.e., 1 followed by 100 zeroes.

FAST FACT . . .

The Googleplex is the corporate headquarters complex of Google Inc., located at 1600 Amphitheatre Parkway in Mountain View, Santa Clara County, California. It's a combination of the words "Google" and "complex," and a clear reference to the term "googolplex."

The founders of Google wanted to name their search engine "googol" to send a message that they would have those many search results.
The number "googol" was coined by nine year old Milton Sirotta in 1935. He proposed that googolplex was a number that's 1 followed by a googol of zeroes or a hundred zeroes.

93. GO, GO, GO!

Humans are obsessed with speed. It doesn't always matter where you're going if you're going quickly enough. So who is the fastest man?

The title of fastest man ever belongs to Usain Bolt, who ran 100 meters in 9.58 seconds. That puts his speed at around 23.3 mph (miles per hour). This is dwarfed by cheetahs who routinely run at 75 mph. The fastest object on land was the thrust ssc (supersonic car) which traveled faster than the speed of sound at a whopping 763 mph.

FAST FACT . . .
Space is so vast that a relatively small distance in space is also huge. The Earth and the Sun are practically on top of each other by space standards. Yet, this distance is so large that it takes light traveling at 186,282.4 miles per second a full 8 minutes and 23 seconds to reach Earth.

Light travels at the speed of 670 616 629 mph! If you were moving at that speed, you could circle the earth 7.5 times in 1 second!

94. BODY MASS INDEX

How do doctors decide if someone's weight is fine or if some sort of change is necessary? There are many methods used, but a common and simple one is called BMI (Body Mass Index).

BMI was invented by Belgian mathematician Adolphe Quetelet. He defined it as the ratio of body mass in kilograms, to the square of height in meters. Being Belgian, he used kg and m as units.

Let's say a person weighs 150 lbs and is 68 inches tall. BMI = (weight)/(height)^2. This makes their BMI around 23. Based on this BMI, and comparing it to a chart, a doctor decides whether a person's weight is fine or if the person needs to gain or lose weight.

For children, BMI is generally not taken as an absolute measure but compared to others in their age group. Muscular people tend to have a higher BMI, as muscle is denser than fat.

FAST FACT . . .

The largest living animal, the Blue Whale, weighs a whopping 170 tons or 375,000 lbs on an average! Its tongue weighs as much as an average elephant.

95. ISBN

If you've ever been to a bookshop or a library and asked for a particular book, you've probably had a book with a similar title handed to you. With new books coming out by the hundreds every-day, how do you tell them apart?

In 1965, Irish statistician Gordon Foster created a sequence of numbers that could be used to uniquely identify each book for booksellers W.H. Smith and others. He named this the International Standard Book Number or ISBN. ISBNs quickly caught on and the International Standards Organization (ISO) formalized and standardized ISBNs in 1970.

ISO 2108 defines a 10-digit format for all ISBNs. As of January 1, 2007, ISBNs have been expanded to 13 digits. ISBN numbers are unique and specify the publisher, country of publishing, group, and title of a given book. You can flip to the back of this book to see the ISBN number if you want.

FAST FACT . . .
The ISBN number of a book is revised for different editions and variations of a book. This means that an ebook, paperback, and hardback of the same book will have different ISBNs and they will also change with each edition.

96. BARCODE

When you shop at a supermarket, you may have noticed that the cashier has a small machine in his hand. He holds it over your groceries. It emits a red light, goes beep, and the item is automatically added to your bill along with its price, any discounts, and applicable bonus points. This machine is called a barcode scanner.

123 45 678 90 10

Barcode scanners are used to scan data directly from an image into a computer. This data is actually a series of numbers that the computer identifies. Barcodes consist of various black and white lines of different densities. The computer detects the reflected light and interprets it into information. As with everything else, the method of creating a barcode from a given data differs from application to application. There are many different standards of barcodes.

Barcodes have made life very convenient for us by allowing easy organization of data as well as by making supermarket lines move quicker.

97. SCIENTIFIC NOTATION

How far is the Sun from Earth? How fast does light travel? How big is an atom? How many cells does a human body have? How fast are the continents drifting away? The answers to all these questions are numbers that are either enormous or miniscule. While science has no trouble dealing with that, it makes writing them down a chore. So we commonly adopt something known as scientific notation.

The speed of light is written as 3x108m/s instead of 300,000,000 m/s. The radius of a hydrogen atom is 0.000000000025 m, and is written as 2.5x10-11 m. We write the number such that there is only one digit to the left of the decimal point. Then we write x10b, where b is the number of zeroes we need to add. If the zeroes are to be added to the left of the decimal point, then b is positive. If they are added to the right, it is negative.

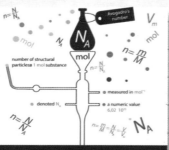

$$N_A = 6,02 \cdot 10^{23}$$

FAST FACT . . .

Avogadro's number is a large scientific number – 6.022×10^{23}. This is the number of molecules in the "mole" of a substance.

98. ZIP CODE

As people moved around the world, they took a piece of home with them, sometimes in the form of culture, but more often in the form of street names or town names that reminded them of their old homes. This made life incredibly hard for postal services that couldn't always be sure where they had to deliver the package. Hence, they came up with postal codes.

FAST FACT . . .
Postal codes can also be a problem. If you type one digit wrong, your mail can land up across the world!

Postal services from all around the world have created their own system of numbering various areas in the country for ease of location and delivery. In the USA, a 5 digit code, called a ZIP code, is used. Most other nations refer to their codes as postal codes or post codes.

The International Standards Organization (ISO) tried standardizing the format of Postal Codes through ISO 3166, but it never really caught on.

99. WHAT'S YOUR NUMBER?

When you have millions of citizens, many of them with the same names and similar jobs who live near each other, how do you keep track of them? Many countries in the world assign a unique number to each individual.

This number acts as a label to distinguish one individual from another. People, too, have number names now! Most countries assign a social security number, or something with a similar name, to the citizen at birth. For example, every Russian citizen has an Insurance individual account number (SNILS). The employment and pension records of each individual are linked to this number.

Every citizen with such a number in these countries is entitled to some citizenship benefits in the form of social security. This means that if they are suffering from unemployment, the state subsidizes their food. They are guaranteed a free primary education by the state and certain basic health benefits.

FAST FACT . . .
Social security codes are also a way for the government keeps track of you through your activities.

100. PERSONAL IDs

Like governments, large organizations often assign numbers to people to easily categorize and organize them. Schools have roll numbers or student IDs, corporate offices have token numbers, and prisons have inmate numbers.

This is most obvious in prison systems or correctional systems in various countries. Once an inmate walks into a correctional facility, he/she is assigned a number.

This numbering process is used in educational institutions as well. Each student is given a certain number which is exclusively assigned to them until they finish their education. This helps them keep a track of the students and their progress. Many official places also do the same for their employees!

FAST FACT . . .

Most militaries worldwide issue their personnel with stamped metallic tags that contain name, rank, serial number, and blood group in case of injury or death. Such "dog tags" are also becoming popular among the youth in many places.

101. WHAT'S YOUR SIZE?

Most clothes and accessories today are mass produced, i.e., made in factories by machines in batches of hundreds or thousands, if not more.

To ensure that everyone gets something that fits them decently, clothing and accessories come in various standard sizes, depending on critical measurements. For example, dress shirts come in various sizes, depending on the width of the shoulder, length of the sleeve, and circumference of the neck. For e.g., dress shirts come in sizes like 40, 42, 44, etc. So a person who measures 41 across the shoulders can buy a size 42 shirt without any discomfort.

The difference between successive sizes varies from apparel to apparel and brand to brand. Except for shoes, it is generally recommended that you go with the next largest size of clothing available. Shoes should be a little tight since they tend to loosen up with use.

FAST FACT . . .

Shoe sizes are generally indicative only of length and do not take into account the general foot shape. This is why people generally insist on trying shoes before buying them.

INDEX